TEEN BEAUTY Secrets

Fresh, Simple & Sassy Tips for Your Perfect Look

Diane Irons

author of *USA Today* bestseller *The World's Best-Kept Beauty Secrets*

SOURCEBOOKS, INC.®
NAPERVILLE, ILLINOIS

Published by Sourcebooks, Inc.
P.O. Box 4410, Naperville, Illinois 60567-4410
(630) 961-3900
FAX: (630) 961-2168
www.sourcebooks.com

Library of Congress Cataloging-in-Publication Data

Irons, Diane.
  Teen beauty secrets : fresh, simple & sassy tips for your perfect look
/ by Diane Irons.
      p. cm.
Includes index.
  ISBN 1-57071-959-4 (Paperback)
  1. Beauty, Personal. 2. Grooming for girls. 3. Teenage girls—Health
and hygiene. I. Title.
  RA777.25 .I76 2002
  646.7'046—dc21
  2002006705

Printed and bound in the United States of America
CH 20 19 18 17 16 15 14 13

TABLE OF CONTENTS

ACKNOWLEDGMENTS

My deepest gratitude and love to my family who patiently wait while I cocoon myself in yet another project.

Thanks to all my friends and colleagues at Sourcebooks for their guidance, patience, and belief in my work.

To Victoria DeMello, my first modeling mentor, one of the most beautiful women in the world, whose charm and elegance I still admire.

To the young women who put their faith in me, I hope my training serves you well.

A NOTE TO PARENTS

There was a time when life as a teen was less complicated. The choices and temptations were there, of course, but there was structure. Did we care about our looks? Of course! We had charm schools to deal with that, working parents were not the norm, and lifestyle challenges were limited.

Having been a teen, modeled as a teen, trained teen models, lived with them, raised them, and been searched out by them for advice, it occurred to me that they are in need of guidance. I remember, before learning from the experts, shaving my brows off, trying to remove warts with acid, and experimenting in the name of beauty with techniques that even I don't want to admit. More than what I did, I have seen unimaginable things happening behind the runway done in the name of beauty that was so underground it should always stay there.

No matter what book I've written, wherever I'm appearing, the concerns of teens come to the forefront. Pimples, when to wear a hat, how to get curly hair straight—the questions and concerns are endless and poignant. Teens enjoy using their looks as a form of self-expression. It's an important way for them to experiment with their independence. A parent may see her daughter in a certain way, the way that she was as a teen, but we must tune into what our teens are, rather than what we would like them to be, or as we see them.

When I became the director of an international modeling agency, I spoke to parents who solely enrolled their teens and preteens in expensive modeling programs in an effort to teach them poise, posture, makeup techniques, and so that they would learn social skills that would take them into adulthood. As an aside, they felt the money was more than worth it when they reflected on their own waste of money and time on clothing styles that were unflattering, and makeup that was totally wrong for their skin type or coloring.

But it goes far beyond covering zits. A teenager is looking to express herself on a daily basis. It's this creative drive that fits in with her lifestyle and individuality. She looks to others to define herself while others look to her in judgment.

That fine line can be crossed at any time. We need to allow for the adventure of change and growth. We need to let our daughters understand that their feelings of trepidation and negativity are normal, that there is no such thing as perfection.

As you continue to build your teen's self confidence, consider my work a blueprint to help in their adventure. Yes, every moment to a teen is a crisis. Even though sometimes talking to our teens is like talking to an alien. I hope this book will help. Don't worry, the breakthrough will come. I hope that this guide will help them to solve some of their beauty dilemmas by searching within themselves and using the tools that will allow them to become strong and beautiful inside and outside, enjoying their birthright. Inner peace can only be achieved with inner confidence.

INTRODUCTION

This is a great time to be a teen. There are more products than ever, individuality is celebrated and accepted, and authenticity is admired. It's also more confusing. With more products, more choices, and fewer rules and guidelines, it's easy to slip from beauty into bimbo.

What's a girl to do? Should I go glam or stay natural? Do I really want to cut my hair? Why did I cut my hair! How do I cover up that zit? I can't go out like that. Why is my tummy so bloated? Am I expecting my period? These are the questions that start around nine or ten and keep going. They last right into your twenties, thirties, forties, fifties, and even longer, but teens have a certain category of beauty that is their very own. No one can appreciate it unless they are going through it. Every generation goes through its own set of beauty problems. Yet, some of these problems carry over from generation to generation—the parent struggle, the not knowing, and the feeling that no one else has ever felt this way.

Surveys have been conducted rating the top three concerns among girls eleven to sixteen. They are appearance, popularity, and self-esteem. Feeling good inside and looking good outside can make life a little easier. It helps by leveling the playing field. You can have fun with beauty, and you can take control of your looks. You and your body, you and your looks can actually become friends.

It is my hope that I have covered as much information as you will need for creating your own style, for feeling comfortable in your unique skin. It's information I certainly needed when I was a teen. I've been working with teen models for a long time and there are formulas and techniques that you can use even if you never step on a runway.

So enjoy the tips, and rather than letting them complicate your life, use them in a way that will bring fun and knowledge.

Chapter 1

ATTITUDE

WHAT ATTITUDE?

This is where you start. The first and most challenging change that I make to anyone—teen, grandmother, preteen—is their opinion of who and what they are. I don't care if I'm working with a girl with braces and weight to lose, or someone ready to hit the runway; it's the same drill. I need to instill the beauty inside before it begins to show on the outside.

TAKE SOME **POSITIVE** STEPS

Look in the mirror and pick out your best feature. If it's your eyes, then keep those eyes in the back of your mind when someone criticizes your calves or points out your pimples or braces.

RESPECT YOURSELF

Unless you do, getting anyone else to is next to impossible. You need to put yourself first in order to keep everything else in perspective.

GET BETTER **EVERY** DAY

Plan to do one thing that will help you improve physically, intellectually, emotionally, even spiritually. Making just one change for the better will boost your attitude from the inside out.

LIKE ALL **YOUR PARTS**

Make friends with every part of your body and face. You can lose weight, you can alter and conceal anything, but your uniqueness will take you through your life. Accept it all, and then you can make the necessary changes to those areas that you like less.

LITTLE THINGS ADD UP

It's amazing, really. The seemingly meaningless things you do for yourself may not have immediate results, but after just a short period of time they'll have you looking and feeling better. So add those bubbles to your bath, make sure you eat your vegetables, and the results will be worth it.

LIVE A **BEAUTIFUL** LIFE

There's a saying that thoughts become things. There's another saying that you wear your spirit on your face. Whether you buy into either philosophy, the more beauty you integrate into your life, the more familiar it will feel.

M I R R O R S DON'T LIE

Catty acquaintances can. Well-meaning friends might out of kindness or fear of hurting the friendship, but if you've got spinach in your teeth, your mirror will point it out.

CONFIDENCE BOOST

JUST **GO**

If you just can't get rid of that cowlick in your hair, that pimple on your nose, or those extra three pounds from yesterday's buffet, just throw some gel in your hair, conceal that pimple the best you can, and wear something that's not too clingy.

BE AN **OBSERVER**

When you see someone who just shouts confidence and beauty, write down what it is about that person that made her stand out. Was it her walk? Her hair? Although it's hard to nail down "polish," there are probably things that this person does that are just a little bit different or better that makes her special.

3

RELY ON YOUR INNER
CHEERLEADER

When you think you can't possibly walk through that door or go out "looking like that," let the person who knows you best, that inner best pal, walk with you.

APPRECIATE

To get that attitude going the right way, you need to appreciate your face and body for what it is.

It may be unrealistic to tell you to love it, but you certainly shouldn't hate it. You definitely need to value what life has thrown you. That's easier said than done in this society of model adulation and unrealistic standards.

LAY THE PROPER
FOUNDATION

Undergarments, a toned body, the right panty hose can make a big difference in the clothing you wear. But even more important is what's in your head when you put on that outfit and when you go out the door. No matter what you're wearing, the right outlook can make the difference in your appearance. That's why models can make the cheapest, plainest piece of fabric look like a couture creation!

SIMPLIFY

LESS **IS** MORE

To feel confident, you don't want to be weighed down with too much "stuff" to worry over. If you've got "dangling this" and "puffed up that," it's too much to control.

If you've got a thick midriff, rather than worrying about sucking in your tummy all day long, it's a simpler solution to wear something loose and flowing and go out with confidence. You can't find a better accessory than confidence and pride.

DON'T MAKE PEOPLE DIZZY

When someone looks at you, give him or her one or two things to admire. More than that and you'll take away from the total effect.

HAVE SOME **PRIDE**

Be proud of who you are. When you have confidence, it shows and makes everything look better.

BE THE STAR OF YOUR SHOW

It's your call. Is your life going to be a drama or a comedy? A musical or a Broadway show? You are the director/producer, and you've got the leading role, so you decide.

What's it going to be? Don't let anyone or anything steal your role.

LIVE WITH IT

Learn to live, even love, everything you have. It's an emotional workout, but worth it. Start chanting, "I love my toes, I love my ears," and soon, you'll believe it. It's probably the most important exercise you'll ever do.

DON'T FORGET **PERSONALITY**

Your personality doesn't have to be outrageous to stand out. You just need to have one. Be sure to use it. It gets stale sitting around. Smile, talk, and get that personality out there so everyone can enjoy it.

SLOW DOWN

Don't let anyone rush you. If someone asks you a question you don't feel comfortable answering, or you just don't have an answer for, just smile and say, "I'll have to get back to you," or, "Let me think about that." Some of the most incredible beauties I know do everything in a slow and deliberate manner. It makes them appear elegant and unshakable. Plus it gives them time to come up with an answer.

EXTRA CREDIT
Think about it. Walking, eating, getting out of a chair, looks so much better when it's done in a more deliberate manner.

SHINE

You need a little glow to be noticed. Of course, you'd like everyone to appreciate your inner spark, but a few highlights here and there on your face, body, or clothing won't hurt a bit. No, don't worry; it won't make you look like Tinkerbell.

JEALOUSY IS A WASTE OF TIME

Remember, nobody's perfect, so what's there to worry about? That person you think has it all together probably has more insecurities than you. Being the best you can be is more than enough.

BLESS YOURSELF

At the end of the day, think of three things that you did well.

STRIKE BACK

If someone hurls an insult your way, do you smile and walk away or let it ruin your day? Do you stand there dumbfounded reaching for words, or do you have a readied comeback: "I can't believe you'd say something like that." "Did those words really come out of your mouth?" Being extra nice is another sneaky attack.

INSTANT ATTITUDE

STRUT A LITTLE

Walk like a model by wearing a slightly raised heel. You'll be more aware of the way you walk, and that's instant attitude. Putting some strut in your walk makes your clothes instantly look better. Lean back ever so slightly, especially if you're wearing pants. It gives you a runway swagger. One foot goes in front of the other. I train models to walk singing a tune in their heads. This is how they find their groove and create their rhythm.

You can do the same, but don't overdo the catwalk style. A little goes a long way.

SMILE

Just doing it makes you happier and more confident. Seeing your smile makes your attitude meter rise.

USE **YOUR** VOICE

The way you sound and the things you say are important parts of that total look.

Your voice has power. You can give your voice the same attitude you give to the rest of your body.

EXTRA CREDIT

Learn to speak from your diaphragm, not from your nose. When I became a broadcaster I had to learn to speak "deeper." What that means is to speak from a deeper part of your body, not from your mouth. A tool used to get more range from singers is to yawn, which stretches out the throat and face muscles.

SHUT OFF THOSE VOICES

When you hear that voice in your head telling you that you're not smart enough, thin enough, pretty enough, shut it off. You deserve to tell yourself only things that will flatter and grow your heart and soul. Tell yourself that being healthy and strong is more important than having rock-hard abs.

TAKE A LOOK **AROUND**

You'll see that the world is not made up of supermodels. Your friends will not win Miss Teen America. It will allow you to put everything into perspective and let you know that you fit right in.

Your curves are functional. Your hips are meant to give birth to children, and your breasts were put there to feed them.

When you look in those magazines don't forget that those models are air-brushed and computer-enhanced. Those actresses have their own makeup artists and hairstylists at their beck and call, all at the snap of a well-manicured finger.

COPY **YOURSELF**

When you find something that really suits you like a great pair of jeans or the perfect shoes, get a couple if you can afford it.

⭐ **EXTRA CREDIT**
Did you get a lot of compliments on an outfit? Take a picture of it, and put it on the inside of your closet. You'll remember it was a hit when you have to put yourself together quickly.

ATTITUDE ADJUSTMENT

TRY SOMETHING **NEW**

Gain a new skill. Learn how to do something better, like learning to lift weights the correct way so that you'll gain more impact and not risk injury.

BE **SAFE**

What? You're telling me to go for it, experiment, and then to be safe? Yes, in your enthusiasm to be a standout, make sure you don't jeopardize your health or safety.

DELEGATE **TIME**

You're worth more than that TV show, and you need to spend a few minutes here and there getting yourself together. Schedule in that time. It will be worth it.

LOSE THE STRESS

Learn to forgive yourself on a daily basis. Stress produces a fight-or-flight trigger. Stress damages your health. It can also ruin your day.

DON'T GIVE IN

Even if you absolutely don't feel like it, make your bed as soon as you get up in the morning. It will start your day off in the right way.

Get dressed and comb your hair. It will make you feel better.

IT'S REALLY USELESS SINCE

Get Rid of Jealousy EVERY ONE

OF US IS UNIQUE. HONOR

THAT SPECIALNESS IN

YOURSELF AND OTHERS.

CHANGE PATTERNS

Changing direction may change your attitude. If you never cared about your underwear, start wearing matching sets. No one will see the difference on the inside, but they'll notice a change on the outside.

BREAK RULES

Beauty rules are meant to be broken. Break them and then put them back together in your own way.

LEARN **NEW** TECHNIQUES

Don't stop learning. Try new things in the privacy of your own home. Ask a few friends to join you. A girl is never too old to play. Use your lipstick to contour your cheeks, try a new face mask, or learn a new dance step.

PUT IT **DOWN ON PAPER**

Write down five things you love about yourself. Are you feeling a little stuck? Ask your best friends to help you out. Write down your wildest dreams and then put it away. Never lose either list.

EXTRA CREDIT
Keep a piece of paper and pencil around so that you can draw pictures of the people, places, and things that make you happy.

ENJOY THE **JOURNEY**

Know that you'll have ups and downs, but don't let it break your stride. There will be good days and bad days. You need to take chances without being afraid to fail. It's like ice-skating. If you keep creeping along, afraid to fall, you'll never really fly free.

Chapter 2

PRE-TEEN
BEAUTY

GETTING STARTED

Between the ages of nine and twelve, things start happening to you that will seem both strange and wonderful. It's called puberty, and it's the beginning of that big adventure into womanhood.

You'll start feeling more grown up, and your figure will begin to change. Some changes will happen gradually while others will seem to "pop up" overnight. Some you'll welcome (like breasts) while others (like pimples and perspiration) will be bothersome. While normal, even expected, these changes can affect your self-esteem. Knowing what to expect and how to handle each situation will make these years easier...and even fun.

TIMING

Everyone experiences puberty at a different time. So if your best girlfriend is getting breasts or has started her period, don't worry. Your time will come. Ask your mother, older sister, or other female relative when she had her first period or started developing, and this will give you an idea when you will begin.

CHANGING & GROWING... ON THE INSIDE

BREASTS

Your breasts will begin to develop as a swelling around the nipple area. They may become sore as well. Don't worry if one grows at a different rate than the other one. They will even out eventually.

⭐ EXTRA CREDIT: **BRAS**

You'll probably be able to sense the right time to start wearing a bra. If your breasts are starting to feel heavy and uncomfortable, then you probably need one. Sometimes a training bra is right for you if your friends develop before you. If it makes you feel better to wear one, then by all means you should feel good about yourself at this most important stage.

GROWTH

You will probably find that your clothes are getting smaller and smaller.

This is because you are going through a growth spurt. You may even reach your final height in this time period. I remember being 5 feet 8 inches tall by the time I was twelve years old. It felt really strange at the time, but seems just right now.

BODY HAIR

Another normal sign of puberty is the appearance of hair in the underarm area, from the lower stomach to between the legs, and heavier growth on the legs. Shaving will become necessary as the hair becomes coarser.

Don't start shaving until you need to. Once you start, you probably won't go back.

SWEATING

Since your glands are also maturing, you'll find that you will be sweating more. You may not feel the need for deodorant or antiperspirant, but a little talcum or baby powder under the arms will help keep the area dry and protect your clothing.

OILY SKIN

This is the time when the skin produces more oils, and you'll find that you need to cleanse your face thoroughly both in the morning and at night. Use a coarse washcloth to ensure that every bit of oil is removed. Allowing the oils to remain on your face will clog the pores and encourage pimples.

GREASY HAIR

You may find yourself needing to wash your hair more often. There are shampoos available in drugstores especially formulated for oily hair that will remove all residues.

You may want to avoid bangs if the oil is concentrated in the forehead area.

EXTRA CREDIT
Concentrate on washing the scalp where the oils tend to accumulate.

CURVES AHEAD

Your hips will begin to spread and get wider while your waist gets smaller. You may find yourself gaining weight in order for your body to make these changes.

FEELINGS

Some of you may want to keep playing basketball, while others may want to experiment with makeup. You may find yourself crying more easily, and getting mad at your parents or siblings more often. Your hormones are making this happen. You may even start thinking that you're weird, or that you're not as normal as everyone else. This is because your personality is developing, and you're starting to look inside yourself.

FRIENDS

Some girls feel more comfortable talking to friends than a parent about their feelings. If this is the case, also consider a teacher, nurse, or guidance counselor. Or, you may want to talk to a friend's mother, a grandmother, or aunt.

CHANGING & GROWING... ON THE OUTSIDE

POSTURE

Don't let the changes your body is experiencing cause you to be embarrassed. Stand up in a way that shows that you are both proud and accepting of these changes, and allow your body to readjust itself and align properly.

UNRULY HAIR

Hair accessories were made for teen hair. Whether you've been scalped or fried by a curling iron, headbands, barrettes, and scrunchies add style and immediate appeal.

SCHOOL RULES

As you begin to experiment with your style, don't forget to check school dress codes.

Most schools ban bare bellies, certain logos, tank tops, and ultra minis. You can definitely look stylish without getting into trouble. Your clothes send an instant message that takes a long time to erase—and you want to send the right message with your style. You don't need to be stuck with a label of what you stand for or who you are when you are still exploring those options.

SHOES

A small heel is fine for daywear if it's worn in a chunky style. Start with a lower heel so that your body gets used to the fine art of balancing.

First Makeup

START WITH FLAVORED LIP BALM—THE CHERRY, STRAWBERRY, AND OTHER FLAVORS GIVE YOU A LITTLE BIT OF COLOR AND POLISH.

SINCE **TODAY'S LOOKS** ARE SHEER,

which looks best on young skin, ask your mom if you can experiment with her eye shadows and blush. Take baby oil or Vaseline and mix it with just enough of the shadow to provide a hint of color wash.

Express your style and go wild with nail polish colors on your fingers and toes. Anything goes here.

Ask your mom, sister, or other family female if you can do her makeup. It's a great way to learn the art of application. Plus, it's lots of fun!

Make your eyelashes stand out by applying a little castor oil to the ends.

EXTRA CREDIT
Don't fall into the trap of putting tons of make-up on at one time. It will look like you're trying to play grown-up.

SUN PROTECTION

Even now, in your "tween" years, you need to wear sunscreen. Most damage to the skin is done before you even hit twenty-five. If you tend to break out from sunscreen, at least wear a baseball cap to keep the sun off your face.

PIERCING

There is nothing wrong with having your ears pierced as long as you take care of them.

While the holes are healing, it's necessary to clean the area with alcohol. Fourteen-karat earrings will help prevent infection. Turn the earrings slightly from time to time while they're in your ear to keep the hole from closing.

OFF THE **BITTEN PATH**

If nail-biting is a habit you'd like to break, this is a great time to do it. It shows that you care about yourself, and that you're no longer a child.

• Keep your nails polished. You won't want to ruin the look. As bad as bitten nails look, chipped nails look worse.

• Use Tabasco sauce or a commercial "No-Bite" product. Both tastes will keep your mouth away from your nails.

• File your nails with an emery board. Ragged, torn nails will only invite you to bite.

• Think about how gross it is to bite your nails and invite all that bacteria into your mouth. Just think for a second where your hands have been!

• Wear a ring or two as inspiration to keep your hands looking nice.

• Apply hand lotion, massaging both hands and cuticles. It's a nice way to relax… and to replace a bad habit with a good one.

GRADE YOUR LOOKS

Look in the mirror and give yourself an "A" for everything that is unique about you.

This includes freckles, dimples, and that beautiful curly hair. This will become your style trademark. It's the path to learning to love yourself as you are.

DRESSING **ALIKE**

When you have a friend who has the same style as yours, it's sometimes fun to wear matching outfits. It certainly creates a major statement and will draw attention to the two of you. Another way of making a statement with a friend is to wear one item alike, like the same skirt with different tops. Fashion should always be fun, and sharing fashion is a great way to start.

FRAGRANCE IDEAS

There are so many ways to use fragrance, and once you start you'll want to use it everywhere, in your bath, on your body, in your room, etc.

It's not necessary to spend a lot of money on fragrance. You can even find it in your own kitchen cupboard, starting with vanilla. Put a little vanilla on your hairbrush, on a lampshade, and even on your clothing.

Go to the supermarket and find great essential oils like lavender (put in or on your pillow to relax), and fruit like lemons and oranges to scent your bath.

Drugstore scents are lots of fun and varied. Plus, the relatively inexpensive prices allow you to experiment.

A **SPACE** FOR YOURSELF

Now is the time to carve out a special area that belongs only to you. Even if you are sharing a room, you at least have your own bureau or a few drawers to yourself. You should be keeping your things together with pride and care.

- Fold your clothes and organize them by color.
- Put small things like socks and underwear in shoeboxes.
- Keep a box under your bed to store items like sweaters and out-of-season clothing.

19

PEP TALK

All around you, girls are changing. Some changes take place gradually, and some seem to happen overnight. Everybody looks different, and that's what's so amazing.

Puberty means growing at different rates, and in different ways.

Right now, taking care of yourself and respecting your body has never been more important.

If you believe you are a beautiful person, then you can face the changes and maintain your self-esteem throughout puberty and your teen years. You'll feel good about yourself no matter what anyone says or thinks about you.

Do good things for your body and yourself. Don't feel you have to look like the girls in the magazines or movies. Beauty comes in all shapes and sizes.

Chapter 3

SKIN CARE

The good news is that half the time you spend worrying about your skin is what it will take to fix it. So stop worrying and start fixing!

DAILY CARE

Creating a skin care routine you can totally handle on a daily basis has never been easier. Now there are products that perform several jobs.

Start your day with a cleanser. It's not necessary to spend a lot on specialty cleansers.

Most teens have oily or combination skin. For this skin type powdered milk mixed with water is my all-time favorite. It's a lactic acid cleanser that will effectively cleanse away the oils while taking off surface debris.

Always use warm water when cleaning your skin, never hot water. Hot water robs the skin of its natural oils. Even teens need some oil to keep their skin balanced.

Toning is the next step. It restores the pH balance to the skin and removes impurities.

Again, don't waste your money on expensive brands. Mixing a teaspoon of lemon juice with ½ teaspoon of tepid water is another favorite, since the lemon shrinks the pores. Also try witch hazel (available at drugstores) or hydrogen peroxide mixed with a little water for very oily skin. These are great toners and won't break the bank like the brand names.

Although it may not seem necessary to use moisturizer for oily skin, a non-oily moisturizer will allow most makeup to go on more smoothly. Most moisturizers also contain some sun protection. If you don't wear makeup, use a sunscreen containing moisturizer.

Use moisturizing gel, not cream, around the eye area, especially if you wear contact lenses.

WOMEN OF COLOR

should be careful not to over-scrub their skin. Unlike lighter skin, irritated dark skin usually doesn't redden, so problems often go unnoticed until they get much worse.

SUN PROTECTION

Do it now, and it will pay off for the rest of your life. Plus your skin will look better even now.

- Use a sunscreen with an SPF of 15 or higher.
- Apply sunscreen about two hours before going outside to give it time to interact with your skin.
- Use common sense in deciding when to reapply. For instance, you'll need to reapply after swimming or sweating.
- Cream is thicker than lotion which means you're going to get more coverage when applying. That's good news for your skin because it will provide better coverage.
- Use products that provide both natural titanium dioxide and synthesized chemicals.
- Avoid the sun between 11 A.M. and 2 P.M. That's when the sun's rays are strongest and most damaging.

ACNE PREVENTION

When the first signs of acne appear, the initial urge is to try to scrub it away. Try your very best to resist, since this just causes flare-ups. Here are some natural ways to reduce and prevent future breakouts.

THE SUN

Laying out in the sun may seem to suppress acne temporarily, but it actually can worsen it. The sun will clog your pores and cause even more pimples. Keep your sunscreen on.

It's important to wear sunscreen rain or shine because sun filters through the clouds.

You may be afraid that **SUNSCREEN** will make your skin oilier, but there are several sunscreens on the market that are especially formulated for oily skin.

YOU PUT YOUR FACE **WHERE?**

Be careful what goes on your face. And I'm not talking that silver neon eye shadow.

Pressing your chin against the phone, resting your hand on your cheek, and touching your face while you're reading can all trigger acne.

TOO MUCH OF A **GOOD THING**

Using too many products and too many ingredients at one time can be worse for your skin than not doing anything at all.

CHIN BREAKOUTS

could be caused by whitening toothpaste. Switching to plain fluoridated toothpaste may help.

ACNE SOLUTIONS

GENTISIC ACID

There's a new acne fighter on the market. Gentisic acid has been found to reduce oil production within the sebaceous glands. Look for this ingredient in several drugstore brands.

START NOW

to read labels before you buy anything. You need to know something about what you put *on* your body as well as *inside* your body.

OVERNIGHT TREATMENT

To dry up a blemish overnight, cover it with a small amount of solid deodorant.

SQUEEZE SAFELY

If you absolutely insist on popping that pimple (and I can't talk you out of it), then let's make sure you do the least damage.

1. Soak a cotton ball in warm salt water. Press on top of the blemish for three minutes. This will dissolve the top.
2. Place cotton swabs on either side of the pimple.
3. Press the swabs toward each until the pimple is flattened.
4. Apply witch hazel to the area immediately.

NATURAL REMEDIES

• Dab garlic juice on developing and mature pimples.
• Pat a drop of honey on the affected area. This deep cleans the pore and draws out bacteria. Keep the honey on for about ten minutes.

YOUR **SKIN** IS NOT THE **SINK**...
don't scrub it too hard!

SKIN TREATMENTS

GET SKIN THAT GLOWS

Start in the shower by washing your skin with an exfoliant. To exfoliate means to slough away dead cells and other debris. You don't want old cells to overstay their welcome.

Place two green tea bags in cool water, then lay them over your eyes for five to ten minutes. Green tea contains strong natural antioxidants.

Dip a washcloth in cold whole milk. Place it on your face for at least fifteen minutes, and then rinse in lukewarm water. Cold milk will calm the skin, and the lactic acid will exfoliate your skin.

OIL ABSORBING MASK

Grind ½ cup oatmeal in a food processor.
Add ½ cup cornmeal.
Add the juice of one lemon to the mixture.
Rub the mixture over the face and leave on about two to three minutes.
Rinse with warm water.
Not only will this mask remove excess oils but will also slough off dead cells.

BLACKHEAD REMOVER

Combine ¼ cup boiling water with one teaspoon Epsom salt and three drops of iodine. Let this mixture cool until it's comfortable to the touch. Soak a cotton ball with the mixture and dab it on the blackheads. This will allow the blackheads to loosen so that they can be easily squeezed or wiped away.

INFLAMMATION-REDUCING COMPRESS

Use this when you have a major breakout or redness.

Prepare three cups of very strong chamomile tea (two teabags to a cup).
Refrigerate in a spritzer bottle for about an hour. You can buy empty spray or spritzer bottles at drugstores and anywhere they sell artificial flowers.
Spray over irritated or inflamed skin.

SPECIAL CONCERNS

CHEST ZITS

Perspiration in the chest area makes it susceptible to pimples. To prevent this, try to wear natural fabrics like cotton, which allows the skin to breathe. Wash the area morning and night just as you wash your face (with an exfoliant like powdered milk or raw sugar).

Once a week apply a mask to clean out the pores. There are inexpensive masks at drugstores, or you can mix your own.

TATTOOS

The problem with tattoos is that once they're exposed to the sun, they fade and turn an unflattering gray. Put the highest SPF sun block that you can find when they will be exposed.

 **EXTRA CREDIT**
Black ink is the least likely to fade.

CELLULITE

Products containing seaweed and caffeine are the most effective, but expensive.

What these products do is temporarily swell the skin, taking away the lumpy bumps.

You can do this treatment at home. Just take some warm coffee grounds and rub them into your cellulite-prone areas. Then cover the area (it should be wet from the grounds) with seaweed.

Let it sit on the area for about ten minutes.

This treatment has been used forever by models and pageant contestants. If you can't afford or can't get seaweed, then use plastic wrap.

EXTRA CREDIT
You can purchase seaweed at natural supermarkets and health food stores.

Exercise and eating right are also very important in controlling cellulite. (See chapter 11, "Body Challenges," for more information.)

Skin brushing also helps. Use a coarse washcloth, loofah, or massage mitt.

SCARS & **STRETCH MARKS**

There are over-the-counter pads that will soften, flatten, and lighten pink and red scars and stretch marks. The success rate is quite high (about 90 percent).

EXTRA CREDIT
Brands to watch for: Regenetrol, Curad Scar Therapy

WHITE BUMPS

Usually they're located on your arms. They look like little zits, but they don't pop.

They are an allergic reaction called keratosis pilaris. It usually clears up in a week, but you can speed things along by using a baking soda and water mixture on the area.

QUICK SKIN FIXES

SCALY SKIN AND RASHES

Vegetable shortening like Crisco applied to the skin will calm down rashes and deeply hydrate skin. Hospitals even use it for treating psoriasis and eczema.

Milk and yogurt applied to the skin will lessen reddening.

RUNNING OUT THE DOOR

If you have just a few seconds to get out the door, a little witch hazel followed by a tinted moisturizer will save the day.

BABY WIPES

Use them to quickly remove makeup and refresh your face.

MEDICAL ALTERNATIVES

If your acne is at the point where it's no longer manageable, you may want to see a dermatologist. There are many different treatments available, and your doctor will determine whether your treatment should be oral, topical, or both. Plus, she will monitor your progress and change treatment techniques when necessary.

RETIN-A

This is a prescription cream, mostly for mild to moderate acne, which unplugs follicles and stops them from clogging.

CORTISONE

This is a heavy-duty shot your dermatologist can give you that will get rid of the blemish right away. It should be saved for very special occasions, like a prom.

GOOD BEHAVIOR FOR GREAT SKIN

EXERCISE

Get a healthy glow by oxygenating the tissues of your skin with regular exercise.

Don't wear a lot of makeup while you're exercising so that your skin gets a chance to clean out and "breathe."

SLEEP

Your skin rejuvenates itself in the last stages of sleep. If you're sleeping less than eight hours, you're not allowing your skin to repair itself.

A **LITTLE** FAT

You need essential fatty acids in your diet to feed your skin. Some of the models I have worked with are guilty of not having enough fat in their diet because they're afraid they'll gain weight, and it really robs their skin of its glow.

READ LABELS

Check expiration dates and ingredients, and follow directions for best results from your skin-care products.

HOW TO USE A **MASK**

Masks are fun to use and can help clean pores, absorb oils, and give the skin a radiant glow.
1. Wash your face. Masks work best when they're applied to clean, dry skin.

2. Follow directions. Don't keep a mask on longer than suggested. Not keeping it on long enough will be a waste of money and time.

3. Rinse your face thoroughly with warm water after removing your mask.

REMOVING MAKEUP

Don't use an oily makeup remover, especially around the eye. If you have to use one with oil (for instance, to remove waterproof makeup) mix it with water before applying.

TRICKS OF THE TRADE

DROWN THAT ZIT

If you really need to get rid of blemishes quickly, apply your treatment up to six times a day. You want to keep the active ingredients working hard for you.

HEMORRHOID CREAM

It takes down the swelling of the pimple.

EYE REDNESS DROPS

It takes the redness out of the pimple and should be used with the hemorrhoid cream to cause the pimple to become invisible.

TEA TREE OIL

A highly effective and natural antiseptic for breakouts. Tea tree oil is the least drying acne fighter, so you won't end up with a dry flaky patch afterward.

BENZOYL PEROXIDE

It's an extra strength product that prevents pimples, since it helps unplug oil and dirt from pores. Find it at drugstores in its pure form and in pimple-fighting cleansers. Don't use too much, or you'll end up with peeling and dryness that will make your face look worse.

OIL-FREE MOISTURIZERS

They do the job without clogging the skin. Use them when skin is most oily (like when you're pre-menstrual), and under makeup.

OIL-BLOTTING PAPERS

If during the afternoon your nose turns into a wet ski slope, you'll be glad you're carrying them in your purse. All you do is press the tissue against the oily spots and let it absorb away!

CULTURAL SKIN DIFFERENCES

Your ethnic background does make a difference in how you should care for your skin and your own unique skin problems.

FAIR

If you have this type of skin, you probably freckle easily and burn quickly.

Fair skin has less melanin, which protects the skin from damage, so it's important to wear a high SPF sunscreen. Be cautious in your choice of skin care, since your face is easily reddened. Due to genetics, you're ten times more likely to get acne.

LIGHT BROWN/YELLOW

The good news is that you usually tan without burning. The bad news? Your big complaint is that your skin tends to look sallow. To get more color into your complexion, use an alpha hydroxy wash and alternate warm and cold water when cleansing.

Since this skin type has more oil glands, watch out for extra shine. Use exfoliants on a regular basis to keep oil at bay.

Take a Minute

TO DO A **QUICK FACIAL**

Dip a washcloth in very warm water and apply it over your face for about thirty seconds. Quickly apply your favorite face cream to lock in the moisture.

TO FIX **YOUR LIPS**

Apply udder balm or petroleum jelly on your lips, and gently rub with a toothbrush or washcloth.

TO HEAL A **PAPER CUT**

Apply a drop of super glue. Then dab on petroleum jelly.

TO GET RID OF **CHAFING**

Apply cornstarch directly from the box to the friction points (parts that rub together). Cornstarch is an anti-chafing, extreme moisture-absorbing powder.

OLIVE/BROWN

You have skin that almost always tans and rarely burns. Those with this skin type usually have to deal with oiliness.

Since your skin type contains lots of melanin, you don't have to worry as much as your lighter-skinned sisters about sun protection, but you still need it. The sun will cause your glands to overproduce oil.

Look for oil-free sun block with an SPF of 15.

DARK BROWN/BLACK

Even though you're less likely to have breakouts, you still need to be careful.

Keloids, which are thick scars, are common to your skin type. Even one pimple can cause inflammation, which can result in a lumpy scar. It's made even worse if you pick at it.

Be cautious about using harsh cleansers and exfoliants since they can cause pigmentation discoloration.

For women of color, it seems that every blemish turns into a dark mark. Many women think it's a scar, but dermatologists say that it is more likely post-inflammatory hyperpigmentation. It's caused by irritation. Don't try to treat it with products containing benzoyl peroxide. Although it's fine for lighter skin, it can increase pigmentation on darker skin. Clear up the dark spot with a mild exfoliant like sugar and olive oil. You should do this to prevent scarring too.

SKIN OFFENDERS

HANDS **AND** FINGERS

As tempting as it is, when you pop, pick, or poke at a pimple, it increases the inflammation and can make your skin even more red and swollen. If you are too aggressive, you could be left with permanent acne scars.

Covering Up

USE A SMALL EYELINER BRUSH to dab on concealer in a shade that matches your foundation.

DIP A SMALL BRUSH, first into loose powder, and then into foundation.

WIPE AWAY EXCESS MAKEUP around the blemish with a cotton swab. If you don't, it will only bring attention to it.

LIGHTLY BRUSH POWDER on top and around the blemish to set it and let it flow into the skin.

IMPROPER **CLEANSING**

Get the oils off with proper cleansing and rinsing morning and night.

OILY HAIR

Believe it or not, the oil from your hair can clog pores. Shampoo frequently, paying attention to the hairline to keep greasiness to a minimum. Keep hair off skin.

HAIRSTYLING PRODUCTS

Some can contain chemicals that get into pores, then clog and irritate them. Try to cover your face when applying them.

COSMETICS

Look for cosmetics that are oil-free and non-comedogenic. Also look for ingredients like clay, witch hazel, and talc. These smooth over and close up pores.

THE TELEPHONE

If you've been breaking out around your chin, look no further than your telephone. It's a breeding ground for bacteria. Wipe down the mouthpiece with alcohol pads every day. Try to break the habit of holding the receiver against your chin.

EXTREME DIETING

Crazy dieting damages the skin because it causes the body to turn to vital organs to get its nutrients. I can tell if a model has been dieting to extreme by the condition of her skin.

SMOKING

Your skin needs oxygen. Smoking deprives your skin of it. Everyone knows that smokers' skin is sallow no matter how young you are. The good news is that quitting will repair your skin quickly.

Skin Care Terms

ACCUTANE
A drug that forces skin cells to mature and flake before bacteria can form.

HUMECTANT
Attracts water from air into skin.

HYDROCORTISONE
Calms redness and acne flare-ups. Also a strong antiseptic.

PETROLATUM (PETROLEUM JELLY)
Seals moisture into skin with a protective film. Commonly found in cold creams and cosmetics.

Chapter 4

PERSONAL STUFF

When it comes to personal grooming and hygiene, this is where teen girls are done a great disservice. There is not a great deal of information out there, especially in the area of disaster control. Its importance can't be overstated.

PRIMARY CARE

Real beauty begins before the makeup, the clothing, or the jewelry. It happens in the privacy of your own home. It can be a party for you, or it can be pure drudgery. I'd go with the party. It will become a fun and much-anticipated event. Plus, it will go a lot faster.

PARTY TIME

Pick a time of day when you can relax. Choose a time when you're not rushed.

As silly as this sounds, it's important to give yourself the time to retreat and restore.

The end of the day usually makes the most sense. But you may choose to do this after class as a way to destress.

GATHER UP YOUR TOOLS

Here's your supply list. A laundry basket makes an inexpensive container. Plus, you'll have everything right at hand, in one place, and ready to use at a moment's notice.

- Fluffy washcloths
- Deodorant soap
- Facial soap
- Fragrant candles
- Scented oils
- Razors
- Tweezers

EXTRA CREDIT
If you have room, add a bath pillow to cushion your neck and head while you're relaxing in the tub.

ODOR PREVENTION & CURES

How do you know when you need odor prevention? It usually begins when you think you do.

There are several varieties of odor protection. Choose whatever is convenient for you. There are liquids, creams, roll-ons, powders, and even soaps to help prevent odor and to keep you dry.

Before you start using a deodorant, you can get away with using just talcum powder under your arms. If you find that you can get away without a deodorant, you might try one of the natural rock deodorants. It's easy to use, you just roll it on, and it's reusable. It contains no chemicals, and is a good way to begin this important intimate routine.

BODY ODOR

Nobody likes to talk about it, and certainly no one wants to have it.

Body odor is not always the result of poor hygiene. It could be that your deodorant is not doing its job for you. When choosing your deodorant, be sure to read labels. Look for the ingredient zirconium aluminum, which is more effective than those containing aluminum chloride. You should also really like the scent of the deodorant, or you'll be better off choosing unscented.

The difference between a deodorant and an antiperspirant is simple. A deodorant covers up odor from any perspiration, usually with a fragrance. An antiperspirant actually plugs the opening of armpit sweat glands so that the perspiration never reaches the skin's surface. Some health experts recommend using a deodorant so that you don't stop your body from sweating, which is natural and healthy. Others state that it won't hurt you to stop the action of a few sweat glands since you've got so many all over your body.

Check with your health-care provider if you'd like more information.

UNDERARM ODOR & WETNESS

The best time to apply a deodorant or antiperspirant is after a shower or bath so that your body will not have had time to develop sweat. Make sure that the area under your arm is completely dry before applying your deodorant so that its strengths will not be diluted in any way.

Always be sure to wait a couple of minutes before dressing so that the deodorant or antiperspirant doesn't rub off on your clothes. Depending on the weather and your level of activity, it's possible to work up enough of the sweat later in the day that you might need to reapply your products.

A LITTLE POWDER

over your deodorant will keep the deodorant secure, and your underarms dry.

BATH TREATMENTS

Bathing is the perfect time to relax and perform your beauty treatments—it's a little like being in a spa but without having to pay the cost. Plus, bathing can do such wonderful things for your skin, your psyche, and your looks.

DID YOU KNOW?

Bathing has been known to lift depression and helps you sleep. A soothing bath has been known to relieve menstrual cramps.

ADD SOME SALT

Go to the grocery store and pick up some sea salt. You'll find it in the baking aisle along with everyday salt. It will become a new beauty product for you. Each time before you step into the bath, take two teaspoons of sea salt and add it to a teaspoon of vinegar. Massage this mixture on dry legs before stepping into the bath.

Don't worry about the salt being in your bath. Salt will help keep your bath water warm for a longer period of time. Why? Salt slows the transfer of heat from the water to the air.

⭐ EXTRA CREDIT

If you suffer from oily skin, cut up some over-ripe lemons, oranges, or grapefruits. Citrus acids kill bacteria and removes impurities. They dry up any excess oil. You'll love the way it smells. It's the ultimate aromatherapy!

YOU NEED TWO SOAPS IN THE BATH

- A deodorant soap for your genitals, feet, and underarms (areas where you perspire)
- A facial soap for your face, arms, and legs

TOWEL TIP

Here's a secret to toweling off. Put some body lotion on a washcloth and pat yourself dry, starting at your feet and working your way up. This spa secret seals in the moisture from your bath and leaves your skin silky smooth.

41

SHOWER POWER

A shower invigorates and is the most efficient way to cleanse.

CLEANSER

Since showering is a daily event (sometimes more than once), all that hot water can be very drying to your skin. To keep your skin moisturized and smooth, use a moisturizing cleanser (like Dove).

For areas that perspire (underarms, feet, etc.) you'll need a deodorant soap.

Don't use such a soap on your face, however. The cleanser you use for your body is not made for your face. Your face doesn't perspire, and it is just too tender for body soap.

TEMPERATURE

Water should not be too hot or too cold. Hot water not only raises body temperature and makes you tired, it dries out your skin, which will make you itchy. Cold water just won't do a proper cleaning job.

WORK YOUR **MUSCLES**

Apply a thin film of bath oil over your shoulders and neck, and drape a towel over your shoulders. Let the towel's heat allow the oil to penetrate and relax your muscles.

SMOOTH YOUR SKIN

Use raw sugar to scrub down your body in the shower. Your skin will glow. You can find raw sugar sold in grocery stores (right next to the regular stuff).

TREAT YOUR **LIPS**

While you're showering, coat your lips with some petroleum jelly. Let the steam hydrate your lips, and then rub the flakiness off with a wet, warm washcloth.

BRUSH AWAY

Take a vegetable brush and brush your entire body with sweeping strokes. You can buy a vegetable brush in hardware stores or in grocery stores. You'll rev up your circulation, and get rid of dry skin. But don't rub too hard—you'll end up with big red rashes. Not a good look!

SPA SECRETS

If you've never been to a spa, you've missed out on some amazing pampering and indulgence. But who says that you should have to spend hundreds of dollars on treatments, when you can accomplish the same thing in your own home?

STONE THERAPY

Gather up some dark stones as you prepare for one of the best treatments available in spas today. Flat stones are preferred because they hold the heat for a longer period of time. It is this heat that helps to reduce high-tension areas. Pick the smoothest rocks you can find, and boil them to a very warm, comfortable temperature. Place them between your toes. Rub them all over your feet, and place them on any stress points that you might have, like your shoulders.

SCALP TREATMENT

Rub your entire scalp briskly, use your knuckles and your fingertips. Grab handfuls of your hair near the roots. Then gently pull your hair for ten seconds. Do this all over your scalp.

SPA POSTURE EXERCISE

I often have my models perform the following exercise in order to teach them to walk more gracefully as well as to improve their posture.
1. Raise your shoulders as high as you can.
2. Drop them quickly, and breathe out forcefully.
3. Do this about four or five times.

GRACEFUL HANDS

Fill a small bowl with warm water, a teaspoon of Epsom salt, and a few marbles.

Get your hand into the water and roll the marbles around. Although I use this exercise to give my models a sense of grace with their hands, you'll find it is a great treatment for fingers that have been typing away on a keyboard all day.

TAKING IT OFF

SHAVING

Soak your skin in warm water before shaving, or shave during or after a bath or shower. Your skin will be softer and you'll get a closer shave.

Spread hair conditioner or shaving cream on the areas you want to shave. This will allow the razor to glide more easily and not knick or cut your skin. If you prefer to use soap, make sure to use a moisturizing soap.

Be sure to soak your skin in warm water before shaving. Or, if you can, shave during or after a bath or shower. Your skin will be much softer and the hair will be that much easier to cut.

Always shave up the leg, not down. Use long, slow strokes. If you shave too quickly you'll end up with nicks and cuts. Be especially careful around very sensitive areas like the ankle and the knee.

Use a moisturizer on your legs after shaving to cut down on skin dryness and irritation.

DON'T SHAVE RIGHT AFTER GETTING OUT OF BED. Your skin is puffy in the morning and the stubble will be less visible.

If you want to make a shave last a long time, use a coarse washcloth or a loofah to scrub your skin before shaving. What you are doing is shedding the top layer of dead skin and removing any oil or perspiration which would prevent you from getting a very close shave.

Leave the very hard-to-shave spots for last. Areas like the back of the knees need a chance to soften. If you go over them too quickly, you'll most likely give them a few little nicks and cuts.

Use hot water to rinse shaving cream or soap from your blade. Use cool water to rinse legs after shaving.

Use a very light touch while shaving. You don't need a lot of pressure, which will dig into the skin and cause cutting.

TOSS YOUR
RAZOR

or change your blades after every four or five shaves.

WAXING

If you are taking an acne prescription like Retin-A or Accutane, check with your doctor before waxing. Medications like these can make the skin very sensitive. Waxing may not be for you.
Avoid waxing the week before and during your period. Your skin is more sensitive at that time.

Further minimize pain by trimming hair that is an inch or longer before you wax. Hair that is too long will hurt when it is pulled.

Hair that that is less than one-quarter of an inch is too short to wax.

Always try to wax in a straight line. Try putting on a bikini bottom or underwear and wax hair that extends beyond the edges of the fabric.

A good way to grab stray hairs is to use a small piece of tape.

If you change your mind about waxing and the wax has already been applied, just shower it off with warm water.

Waxing Tips

•**TAKE AN ASPIRIN** before you wax to help minimize swelling.

• Use a **COLD WAX** instead of a hot one. Less heat means less redness.

• After waxing, apply an **ANTIBIOTIC** like Neosporin. Avoid applying anything containing alcohol, which can sting.

• Apply **MILK OR YOGURT** compresses to sensitive areas after waxing.

OTHER HAIR REMOVAL OPTIONS

Chemically removing hair can be irritating to the skin. For this reason you should test a small area on your arm to be sure that your skin is not too sensitive for this type of hair removal.

Most spray-on techniques have an awful smell to them and don't really work well. No one I know uses them on a regular basis.

Laser hair removal is a technique that can be done by a dermatologist. It's very expensive and takes time. If you have an area that is really bothersome (hair on the face, for instance), and you want to have it permanently removed, then it may be worth it.

Sugaring is like waxing. It consists of a sugar paste that's completely natural. It is applied with bare hands.

LOOK!

I know that removing hair is never really much fun. But if you take a little extra time and just a bit of preparation, you'll have a much smoother result.

A WINNING SMILE

To keep teeth and gums healthy, as well as create a beautiful smile, it's important to keep up a daily care regimen. This includes proper brushing and flossing. It's especially important if you wear braces.

FINDING THE **RIGHT BRUSH**

Manual: The advantage is that you control the pressure. Technique makes all the difference—be sure to brush up and down for at least two minutes. Most of us don't brush long enough. While you're at it, brush your tongue. Your tongue has a ton of germs and bacteria that may be causing bad breath.

Electric: This makes brushing both fun and easy. The manufacturers have clinical studies to prove that this type of brushing gets teeth whiter by removing stains.

Its secret is the combination of thirty thousand to thirty-five thousand brush strokes per minute and gentle sonic waves (as in the case of the popular Sonicare line). These are similar to the cleaning instruments used in your dentist's office. Its technology allows an electric toothbrush to remove plaque below the gum.

DID YOU KNOW?

Your toothbrush has more germs than a toilet flush handle. Change your brush every three months.

GET THOSE TEETH THEIR **WHITEST**!

Whitening toothpastes can really help your teeth to get their whitest, but don't overdo it. Some of them are just too strong and may wear off enamel and even cause your fillings to fall out. There are natural and inexpensive ways to whiten your teeth.

First you should know that there are foods that can actually whiten teeth, just as there are foods that can stain teeth. When you eat blueberries, drink coffee or tea, etc., be sure to brush and floss right away so that those stains don't settle in. Try to concentrate on foods that act like detergents and whiten teeth naturally. These are generally the foods that require a lot of chewing like apples, celery, and carrots. There are other foods that act like a barrier on teeth by creating a film. Broccoli, lettuce, and spinach are foods that actually prevent staining from occurring.

⭐ **EXTRA CREDIT: EXTRA WHITENING**

Here's a great way to whiten your teeth and freshen your breath at the same time. All you do is take a couple of strawberries and mash them in a dish or bowl. Then taking your finger spread the pulp all over your teeth. Leave it on a minute or two, and then brush it off thoroughly.

DRUGSTORE WHITENING

Whitening dental gums

These fairly inexpensive gums with bleaching ingredients help give teeth polish.

Regular sugar-free gum can also help brighten teeth by stimulating saliva to take stains from your teeth.

Whitening strips

These are flexible strips that are applied directly to your teeth and contain a very high amount of peroxide similar to the peroxide gel that dentists use during their bleaching procedures. They promise to whiten teeth in two weeks, and the results last up to six months. Plan to spend from $25 to $50 on a package.

RIGHT BEFORE YOU VISIT YOUR DENTIST, apply some petroleum jelly or lip balm over your entire lips so that they won't get cracked or stretched out during the exam.

EVERYDAY WHITENING

As it is with any stain, the longer they stay on, the harder they are to remove. That's why it's important to keep up those twice-a-year dental visits. Smoking and/or drinking dark beverages like coffee or tea also will contribute to staining. It's not practical to carry a toothbrush around with you all day, so try to remember to rub your teeth with a tissue after eating or drinking. This, of course, will not work if you are wearing braces.

FIGHT CAVITIES IN THE SHOWER

Here's a great model trick. When you're in the shower, bare your teeth and let the spray batter your gum line. This massages your gums and removes much of the bacteria that can lead to tooth decay.

FLOSSING

For good teeth, fresh breath, and healthy gums, it's important to floss at least once a day. It removes plaque that gets between teeth and under gums that brushing just can't reach.

When you're at the drugstore you'll see a lot of different flosses to choose from.

Thicker flosses or unwaxed work best for hard to reach spaces in the teeth.

Choose your favorite flavor.

Let your dental hygienist teach you how to floss properly.

BEDTIME MAGIC

What can I say about beauty sleep?

It's true. It really exists, and you need it. Your skin repairs itself while you sleep. It can even help treat conditions like acne and other skin diseases. You just can't look good when you don't get enough sleep, and you can't think as clearly. Teens need more sleep than anyone else because their bodies are still developing and growing. Try to get at least eight hours a night.

Can't sleep? Take some lavender oil and drizzle it on a hanky or cottonball. Place it inside your pillow. You can find it in at herb shops, and natural food stores. Lavender is great for promoting sleep and relaxation.

When you have a cold or your nose is stuffy from allergies, it's sometimes hard to get to sleep and stay asleep. A few drops of eucalyptus sprinkled on a hanky and placed inside your pillow will promote breathing and healthy sleep through the night. Eucalyptus oil usually can be found in natural supermarkets and health food stores. Fresh eucalyptus can be found at most flower markets. A sprig or two by your bedside also may help.

Give your hands and feet a real softening treatment by spreading your favorite moisturizer over them and wearing gloves and socks overnight.

GETTING REALLY PERSONAL

There are some really intimate details you don't want to forget. Most teens don't know where to get answers for these very personal dilemmas.

NIPPLES

Once in a while you might find a hair or two growing around the nipple of your breast. If it's just one or two hairs, it's perfectly OK to pluck them out with tweezers. If you're too nervous to do it, you can shave or cut them off with small cuticle scissors.

A lot of girls want to know if their nipples are normal in size and color. This area, called the areola, ranges in color from very light pink to dark brown. They're as unique as you are.

Another source of concern is when nipples stick in instead of out. This is known as an inverted nipple. Some nipples are flat. Again, this is all normal, and fairly common.

PUBIC HAIR

It's OK to shave or trim this area if it makes you feel better. Just be careful. A mirror might help you do it with more confidence. Plus it's a good idea to get familiar with all areas of your body.

BUTT PIMPLES

What's a girl to do when she has just put on her favorite bikini and found that it's not looking so great back there? Treat butt pimples the way you do facial ones. After all, skin is skin. Use a medicated wash or antibacterial dishwasher detergent in the area.

Another fix is to rub the affected area with a mixture of equal parts of petroleum jelly and vitamin K.

PREVENT

BUTT PIMPLES

by avoiding very tight clothing and by showering after working out.

BODY PIMPLES

Bumps that look like acne, usually located on the upper arms, are caused by clogged hair follicles. Don't pick at them, because that will just make them worse. Use a loofah or rub briskly with a washcloth to allow the skin to breathe.

BIKINI RASH

Very close shaving can make hairs split and loop under the surface of the skin. They push against your skin and cause inflammation and redness. Treat the area with tea tree oil, available at most drugstores or health food stores.

SPIDER VEINS

One reason you may have spider veins is simply because they are hereditary. Injury to the leg, like bumping into something, also can cause spider veins. Purchase vitamin K in liquid capsules. Break the capsule open with a safety pin. Gently tap the liquid on the vein. It has the ability to constrict blood vessels, which will make the vein less visible.

FOOT ODOR

Just like the rest of your body, your feet sweat. In the warmth and moisture of your shoes or sneakers, odor builds up quickly.
- Dust feet with baking soda before socks and shoes go on.
- Rub on alcohol or tea tree oil daily to kill bacteria.
- Try to avoid shoes made of vinyl, which traps perspiration.

Foot Recipe

Brew **EIGHT BAGS** of black tea in one quart of water for fifteen minutes.

Let the water **COOL** until it's comfortable to the touch.

Soak feet for **TWENTY MINUTES**, or until water is completely cool.

The **TEA** contains tannic acids, which kill bacteria while decreasing perspiration.

GAS, FLATULENCE, PASSING WIND (OH MY!)

It's normal, it happens to everyone, but it's embarrassing. Here's what you can do to prevent it.

- Cut down on breads, crackers, and pasta, and try to eat more cooked vegetables. Vegetables that are cooked are easier to digest.
- We've all heard that beans and cabbage can cause gas and bloating, but even bagels can be hard to digest.
- Drink lots of water and chew foods thoroughly.
- Flavor foods with ginger.
- Chew on clove gum.

⭐ EXTRA CREDIT

Models use fennel seeds to keep down their sweet cravings and to keep embarrassing sounds from happening. They chew the seeds or make tea with them.

BLOATING

Eating food too fast, talking while eating, drinking too many sodas, and chewing gum can cause bloating. All bring extra air into the intestines. When this happens, you feel like you have a spare tire around your tummy, or it may feel like you've gained ten pounds overnight.

You can work to prevent bloating by taking smaller bites, and chewing your foods thoroughly, and by avoiding any foods that are either too hot or too cold. Drink chamomile or lemon balm tea to help relieve that bloated feeling.

INTIMATE ITCHING

This uncomfortable feeling often is caused by a reaction to fabric detergent, deodorant soap, perfumed toilet paper, or bubble bath. Reducing exposure to any one of these may solve the problem. Perspiration also can be the problem. Wash with warm water two to three times a day and dust with cornstarch powder.

Eat eight ounces of yogurt a day.

Find relief by drinking warm mint tea.

If the itching persists for more than a few days and/or your discomfort is unbearable, call your doctor.

SCENTS AND FRAGRANCES

Fragrances are so much fun! Using scent is a way to express your mood, and even change it. Changing your scent is easier to change than an outfit, and can be an important part of your personality.

Fragrance seems so simple and yet has so many complications. Even your diet can affect the way a fragrance smells, as well as how long your scent will last. For instance, if you eat an especially spicy diet, your fragrance will become stronger.

TO MAKE YOUR PERFUME LAST EVEN LONGER,

first apply a little bit of petroleum jelly or baby oil where you put your perfume. This gives your fragrance something to hang on to, especially if your skin is dry.

Some girls like to apply perfume on their clothes. Another way to be awash in fragrance is to handwash your hose and lingerie in the sink with a few drops of perfume added to the water.

Make Your Fragrance Last Longer

1. Start by **LAYERING YOUR SCENT** using a scented shower or bath gel.

2. Then **APPLY** a perfumed body lotion while your skin is still slightly damp.

3. To get the most out of your scent, apply it where your skin is warmest. These are your **PULSE POINTS**.

4. Your fragrance is most effective behind your **EARS**, along your **WRIST**, below your **NECK**, above your **CHEST**, behind your **KNEES**, and under your **FEET**. The heat that is generated in these areas keeps your fragrance on longer.

SCENT YOUR **HAIR**

Spray your fragrance on your hairbrush and brush away! Your fragrance contains a bit of alcohol to help hair stay put.

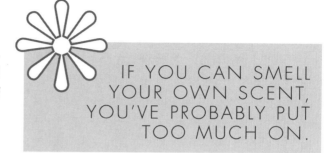

HOW TO SHOP FOR FRAGRANCE

Not all fragrances smell the same on everyone. Take a sample spritz and then walk around for twenty minutes to really see if it's for you.

It takes at least ten minutes after spraying on a fragrance for the alcohol to evaporate and for the scent to blend in with your particular body chemistry

After two or three fragrances, your sense of smell tires out. If you really want to test a bunch of fragrances, bring a package of coffee beans with you and give it a sniff so that you can clear your fragrance palette. Do this after testing two to three scents at a time.

Ask for some samples to take home so that you can really rest your nose between tests.

THAT TIME OF MONTH

What's the best protection to use? Here are your choices.

PADS

Pads come in various lengths and thickness. There are pads for heavy flow. There are pads made for a light flow. Some pads come with adhesive backing that sticks to your underwear. Some pads also come with wings on the side to hold pads in place and to protect your underwear.

57

EXTRA CREDIT
Choose your pad to your flow and how active you'll be during the day.

TAMPONS

These are small pads placed inside the vagina to absorb menstrual fluids. They come in different absorbencies for heavy, medium, and light flows. Some come with applicators to guide the tampons in. Each has a string to pull on to remove the tampon. The string should hang outside the vagina.

Tampons are very drying, and should be used carefully.

PANTYLINERS

These are very thin pads. They're just right for when your period is just beginning or about to end. Some girls like to use them as a backup to their tampons during heavy days.

DON'T

DON'T use a tampon before your period begins to flow.

DON'T leave a tampon in for more than seven hours.

DON'T wear a tampon at night when your period is ending.

TOXIC SHOCK SYNDROME

This is a rare but serious illness which can result from improper use of tampons. If you should find yourself dizzy, developing a rash, or getting a fever or diarrhea, stop using the tampon immediately and call a doctor.

If you find yourself getting your period and you're without a pad or tampon, you can use folded tissues or even toilet paper as an emergency pad.

CRAMPS

Laying flat on your back with your feet up on the wall may help. If you usually have mild cramps but for the last two months they've turned into sharp or severe pain, it's important to speak with your gynecologist.

INTIMATE CHANGES

From about the age of **eight to fourteen**, your ovaries will start maturing. Breasts start to develop, and your nipples start to get darker and grow a little bigger. Hair in your pubic area and under your arms also starts to grow.

Your hips, thighs, and butt will also begin to fill out. This is normal.

Your vagina begins to create a discharge.

Ten to Fifteen
Your body starts developing curves.
Your first period may begin.
Sixteen to Nineteen
Your breasts get to be their full size.
Your pubic hair finishes growing.
You will reach your eventual height.
Your period may also begin at this time.

Gross Growths

WARTS

How do you know if it's a **WART**? Soak the bump in vinegar for several minutes. If it turns white, then it's a wart.

Here's a natural way to get rid of warts. Take a little **GARLIC** juice and apply it to the wart.

Then wrap a Band-Aid around it. It should clear up in a few days. There are also wart solutions sold at drugstores that work well.

IMPERFECTIONS

STRETCH MARKS

Girls usually get stretch marks because skin grows quickly through puberty and subsequently stretches. They start out as red and eventually fade to white.

- Use an exfoliant and moisturizer on the marks.
- Try to keep your weight from going up and down.
- Apply vitamin C to the area.
- Retin-A, available from physicians and dermatologists, has been proven to be helpful.

CELLULITE

Cellulite is another problem that even teens can have. This pesky problem knows no size or age. Even very, very thin models have cellulite.

No. 1:

Treat it with warm coffee grounds. Rub used warm coffee grounds into the cellulite area with a coarse washcloth or loofah. Wrap the area with plastic wrap for a few minutes. Then rinse.

No. 2:

Self-tanning lotion will hide the appearance of cellulite.

SELF-TANNING TIPS

You need a quick tan but you want to look like you spent a week in the tropics.

1. Take off all your jewelry and remove all excess hair.
2. Pull your hair back with a headband. Don't use a shower cap because that will make you perspire.
3. Put petroleum jelly on your lips and brows.
4. Make your self-tanner easier to apply by mixing it with just a bit of moisturizer.
5. Use a cotton swab to lightly apply self-tanner around tricky spots like hairlines, ears, and nostrils.
6. Apply the tanner thinly and evenly. Don't glob it on. You can reapply more later.

7. Don't move around too much after applying. Even quick-drying brands take a few minutes.
8. Don't apply too much self-tanner around the eyes.
9. Use cuticle remover to get tanning stains off your hands.
10. Use a Q-tip to lighten tanner around the hairline.
11. Work in a cool room so that perspiration doesn't spoil your tan.
12. Exfoliate rough areas before applying tanner. Otherwise, the tanner will settle into your skin surface and make the color uneven.

TONGUE BURNS

- Suck on a piece of ice to give you immediate relief and stop tissue damage.
- Gargle with salt water. Take a half a teaspoon salt and put it in a cup of warm water.

- Do this every hour or two to keep your mouth clean and to help heal the burn.
- See your doctor or dentist if the burn hasn't healed in a week.

PIERCING

Don't leave this job to just anyone. Whether you're having your ears pierced, or something more, you get what you pay for.

Mall piercing is OK for ears, but not for other body parts. The jewelry in a mall-piercing gun is a stud, only appropriate for earlobes (definitely not for bellies, tongues, etc.).

A hoop earring is much safer because it allows the piercing to be cleaned properly. This lessens the possibility of infections or other complications.

SUNBURN

Soak in a green tea bath.

Add half a box of baking soda to your bath.

Mist your skin with chamomile tea spritzer.

To prevent a sunburn, always use an SPF 15 or higher.

PREVENT SUNBURN IN THESE AREAS

- Your nose is the most exposed area on your face and the first place to burn.
- Your hands are continually exposed. The back of your hands get sunburned quickly.
- If your ears are exposed, so be sure to dab on the sunscreen.
- If you wear sandals, you risk a burn on top of your foot if you don't apply sunscreen to this area.
- Apply sunscreen directly on the scalp along the part.
- Also use sunscreen around the hairline area, going slightly into the hairline.

Chapter 5

HANDS & FEET

TWO GREAT ASSETS

You don't need to spend a lot of time or money on your hands and feet to keep them looking great. Your hands (especially your nails) and your feet are a great way to make a statement about your style, and they're noticed, maybe more than you may realize. Even more important, they take a lot of abuse (more than any other part of you), and need the attention. Plus, you'll look and feel better.

Nails help us express ourselves. They're like a pretty bow that finishes off a beautifully wrapped present. Nails are a statement that you are presenting yourself to the world in a more together way. It's a great way to say, "I'm grown, polished, and I'm styling."

First comes maintenance, and then comes the pizzazz.

PERFECT NAILS

THE **ESSENTIAL** NAIL KIT

- **Nail clippers**

Allow you to cut nails in sections, preventing tearing.

- **A fine nail file**

Most are unnecessarily harsh.

- **Cuticle stick**

Use a plastic one. Wood retains bacteria, and metal sticks can damage nails.

- **Cuticle oil**
- **Nail buffer with cushioning**
- **Hand cream**

Try to find one with tea tree oil.

- **Polish remover**

Acetone-free remover is less harsh and won't damage nails.

NAIL RULES TO LIVE BY

- Fingernails are not tools. Use a key to open soda cans. Tweezers will pick up small items.
- Wear gloves when washing dishes and other chores which are harsh to hands.
- Don't bite your nails or cuticles. It makes you look nervous and insecure.
- Don't dig around the bottom of your purse or backpack with your nails.
- Tweeze, wax, or shave hairy knuckles.
- Bare nails are better than chipped polish.

FILE NAILS IN A ROUND SHAPE WITH A SLIGHT TAPER TO KEEP NAILS STRONG.

HAND CARE

Dip a nailbrush or toothbrush into warm, soapy water. Polish over and under nails. Pat dry. Gently push cuticles back with a cuticle stick, and remove dirt or residue from under your nails.

EXTRA CREDIT
Leave a little space in between cuticles and nail for a clean, professional appearance.

YELLOWED NAILS REMEDIES

Fill a bowl with warm water. Add ½ teaspoon sea salt and one sliced lime.

Soak hands for ten minutes.

Mix one-tablespoon hydrogen peroxide with two tablespoons of baking soda.

Brush on nails with a small toothbrush.

Rinse immediately.

CUTICLE REMOVER

Scrub excess cuticle away with toothpaste. It works to soften and remove them.

Finish up by rubbing petroleum jelly or bag

balm (available in the skin care section of most drugstores) to lock in moisture and soften rough edges.

SOFTEN HANDS

Warm some olive oil and soak hands

for ten minutes. Rinse and pat dry.

POLISH TRICKS

Avoid quick-drying polishes. They have a large amount of acetone, which dries out polish and causes cracks. Use regular polishes instead for a manicure that will last three times longer.

Prevent bubbles by prepping nails with witch hazel.

Always roll polish, never shake the bottle, or you'll be sure to get bubbles.

Just roll the bottle between your palms. That's more than enough to mix polish.

Dip nails in ice water for ten seconds to set color.

Remove polish stains by soaking nails in white vinegar for ten minutes.

Store polish in the fridge for a longer life.

One coat is all you need of light polish. Most darker colors require at least two coats.

Don't do more than three strokes to each nail.

STEADY YOUR HAND BY RESTING YOUR PINKIE ON A COUNTER OR DESK.

START AT THE MIDDLE OF THE NAIL AND MOVE TO THE SIDES.

USE POLISH THINNER, NOT REMOVER, TO EXTEND THE LIFE OF YOUR OLD POLISH.

MAKE YOUR MANICURE LAST:

• Buff before polishing to smooth down the nail surface.

• Make sure your nails are totally dry before applying polish.

• Keep coats as thin as possible. Thicker coats peel faster.

• Never soak nails before applying polish. The moisture will remain and cause the polish to lift.

GIVE YOURSELF A FRENCH MANICURE

The French manicure is one of the most sought-after looks. It looks natural and fresh, and if done right, very classy. It also costs a lot to have it done professionally, and just as much for the upkeep. In just five easy steps, and in just minutes, you can give yourself a professional-looking French manicure. Don't worry if you don't get it perfect the first time. Just keep at it. You'll soon become an expert.

• Apply a base over clean, buffed nails.

• Follow with one or two coats of natural pink or nude color polish.

• Holding the end of a nail file almost to the edge of your nail, sweep a line of white polish across the entire tip. Try to do it in one stroke.

• Follow up with another coat of your first polish, covering the entire nail, including the white edge.

• Finish with a topcoat to provide shine and protection.

Longer, Stronger Nails

Are your nails constantly chipping, peeling, and breaking? Here are three fast fixes.

• Massage **GARLIC OIL** into the nailbed and cuticle.

• Look for a **NAIL HARDENER** with calcium. Don't forget to apply under nails too.

• Rub **HAIR CONDITIONER** into your nails. It contains proteins to strengthen nails.

FABULOUS FEET

START WITH **SOFT SKIN**

Fill a basin with warm water and add the juice of a lemon with one cup of oatmeal.

Soak feet for ten minutes. While soaking, rub the oatmeal on your feet. The oatmeal will soften rough feet and the lemon will lighten and even out skin.

File rough spots with a coarse nail file.

APPLY VICK'S VAPORUB

on dry feet before bed. Wear socks, and your feet will be smooth and silky the next morning.

FOOT **MASSAGE**

Apply any oil, and gently rub the tops, side, and bottoms of your feet in circular movements using both your thumbs and fingers.

THE **PERFECT** PEDICURE

File nails straight across. You don't want to risk ingrown toenails or weaken your nails.

Remove moisture by swiping rubbing alcohol over the nail bed.

Push back cuticles.

Prep with a base coat. Place tissues between toes to prevent smearing.

Apply polish, starting with the smallest toe.

Apply two coats, waiting five minutes in between coats.

Wait five minutes more and then apply topcoat.

Erase any mistakes with a cotton swab dipped in polish remover.

PLEASE DON'T!

Wear open-toed shoes or sandals without manicured feet.

Even if you like your nails natural, you still need a gloss over them to protect and strengthen them.

MAINTAIN

your manicure by applying a lotion to your nails and hands daily.

KEEP YOUR FEET SWEET

Make sure your footwear fits properly. You need room in your shoes and socks to wiggle your toes.

FOOT EXERCISE

Rub your foot over a soda can or a tennis ball to help cramps and to relax feet.

NAIL ART

Glue a charm to the nail when polish starts to set. Follow with a clear polish to help it stick.

PEDICURE RULES

- Start with soft skin.
- Smooth any ridges.
- Never apply lotion between toes because moisture there can lead to skin fungus.
- Don't shave off calluses and corns with a razor. Just put a little muscle into your nail file.
- Always wait an hour before putting shoes back on.

FOOT PROBLEMS & SOLUTIONS

CORNS

What are they?

Red, thick skin on tops of toes or between toes.

Soak feet in warm salt water.

Buff with a coarse emery board.

Apply a pineapple slice for five minutes over

the corn. The enzymes will further dissolve the corn.

Rub in lotion and sleep with socks.

If the corn is really thick, see a podiatrist (foot doctor).

BLISTER

What is it?

A large, watery pimple.

Don't pop it, or it may cause an infection.

Apply antibiotic ointment and cover it with a cushion bandage so it will avoid friction with your shoes.

CALLUSES

What are they?

Patches, usually white, of hard, thick skin that rub against shoes and cause discomfort and burning.

Soak in a teaspoon of dishwashing detergent and two tablespoons olive oil mixed into a quart of warm (not boiling) water.

INGROWN TOENAIL

What is it?

Pain and swelling where the edge of the nail curls into the skin.

Soak it in warm water and Epsom salts.

Wear sandals or wide box shoes (square toes) to relieve pressure.

If there's pain or pus, see a doctor.

PLANTAR WART

What is it?

A wart under your foot. When you have one, it feels like you've stepped on something.

There are over-the-counter treatments sold at most drugstores.

You can temporarily relieve the pain by rubbing ice on the area, or rolling a can of cold soda under your foot.

If it's deep, see a podiatrist or dermatologist.

HEEL SURVIVAL

Don't wear heels every day.

Change styles so that your feet will hit the ground at different pressure points.

Go up half a size to allow for comfort and swelling.

Replace plastic heel tips with rubber for relief and safety.

Chapter 6

BEAUTY ON A BUDGET

Once you find that you can look great for little money, you won't want to spend an extra penny. There are ways to look as good if not better than those who spend a fortune on beauty. Whether it's beauty or fashion, there's no need to break the piggy bank to look great.

SHOPPING

HIDDEN TRAPS

When you're shopping you should know that there are things that stores do to make you want to buy, and then buy some more.

- They will play relaxing music.
- There will be scents that will make you want to stay, relax, and buy.
- The colors will make you pay more. Pink is the No. 1 favorite of packaging experts.
- The item you're most likely to pick will be at your eye level or lower.
- It will be priced right. Nine is the most popular final digit. It makes the buyer think she's getting a good deal.
- It's touchable. Buyers like to feel fabrics before buying.
- There will be a coupon to cinch the deal.

WHAT YOU NEED TO DO TO TAKE CHARGE

- Shop with a list. You need certain things. A list will keep you from getting sidetracked.
- Compare prices. Try to get the best deal.
- Use a three-way mirror. You want to look great at every angle for anything you wear to be truly worth buying.
- Don't let salespeople make you buy anything. You know what looks good on you.
- Find things that are easy to care for. Check the labels for instructions. If something is a good buy, and constantly has to be sent to the cleaners, it's a budget-breaker.
- Don't buy anything that pulls, bunches, rides up, or makes noise when you walk.
- You should be able to pull an inch of fabric

away from you to allow you to eat, move, and be comfortable.

DRUGSTORES

You can save big money plus avoid being hassled or ignored by counter chicks by shopping in drugstores for your beauty stuff. The cosmetics at the department store counter are often made with the same technology as the drugstore brands. Some are even made in the same factories, and owned by the same parent companies. The only differences are packaging, marketing, advertising, sales help, counter leasing, and, of course, price.

HAIR PRODUCT

like shampoos and conditioners from drugstores are fine. Some are highly concentrated and are best used on damp hair. Read the directions.

DRUGSTORE FINDS

PETROLEUM **JELLY**

- Use it to moisturize your lips
- It's a great highlighter on cheekbones
- Add it to powder eye shadow to create an eye gloss.
- Spread it on cracked heels and rough knees.

BABY WIPES

Yes, you do have a reason to use these even when you're *not* baby-sitting. Baby wipes can remove makeup, clean stains, and, in a crunch, they make great skin refresheners.

COTTON SWABS

- Fix makeup mistakes
- Emergency makeup applicator
- Mixing colors

Finding the Right Shade without Opening the Bottle

CHECK THE LABEL

You'll see brief descriptions that will help you decide.

Most drugstores have shades that can work on a range of skin tones, so you can feel safe going a little lighter or darker. If you're stuck on whether to go lighter or darker, go lighter if you don't wear powder. Go darker if you like to wear powder. Setting powder over your foundation will make it look a bit lighter.

HOLD THE BOTTLE TO YOUR JAWLINE TO GET THE CLOSEST MATCH

Try to go the nearest and biggest window in the store. If you can't, then put your face and the bottle in a mirror.

GROCERY STORE BEAUTY

You can find great stuff in the kitchen, or at the grocery store.

WOULD YOU RATHER?

PAY $20.00 FOR A MILK CLEANSER OR $1.29 FOR A BOX OF POWDERED MILK?

The only difference is that you mix the powder with a little water.

PARSLEY

Get the dried variety or the fresh stuff. Put a teaspoon of the dried flakes in a cube and freeze it. Use it to get rid of the swelling in a pimple. Take a sprig of fresh parsley and chew it on your way out the door. Parsley is packed with chlorophyll, which is the major ingredient in breath mints.

LEMONS

Use the juice of a lemon mixed with an equal amount of water. It's a great oil-reducing facial toner.

Cut one up and put it in your bath for super clean skin, and absolutely natural aromatherapy.

VEGETABLE BRUSH

Don't spend a lot on body brushes. A vegetable brush buffs away dead skin and gives a great glow at an affordable price. Use it on dry skin just before showering.

BAKING SODA

Add enough water to baking soda to make a paste and apply it to blemishes overnight. It will dry them up by morning.

Add it to your toothpaste to get rid of tartar and to whiten your teeth.

KOSHER/SEA SALTS

Add your favorite essential oil to ½ cup of this coarse salt to make inexpensive bathing salts.

Almond oil is a great choice. Or you might choose vanilla. You can even add a little food coloring. These make great gifts.

★ EXTRA CREDIT

Use salt on your scalp to get rid of dandruff. Before shampooing, massage your damp scalp with about a tablespoon of salt.

GREAT HAIR FOR LESS

HAIRCUTS

Here's a great way to get a great cut and spend little or nothing. Call around to large salons and ask if they have an apprentice or training night. If they do, that means you'll get a huge discount on cut, color, and blow dry. Don't be afraid, every trainee is totally supervised.

HIGHLIGHTS

So you say you want to put highlights in your locks, but there's that expense thing or, even more important, parental approval blocking your way? Do it gently with vinegar!

I'm serious. Flavored vinegars can enhance and even create subtle highlights. You just choose the vinegar to match your hair.

Pale blonde...white vinegar
Deep blonde... balsamic vinegar
Strawberry blonde...raspberry vinegar
Dark hair...red-wine vinegar

Add five tablespoons of vinegar to your shampoo. Leave it on for ten minutes. Rinse. Condition if you need to. This solution is also great for shine and squeaky-clean hair.

EXERCISE ON A BUDGET

You don't have to join an expensive gym to get your exercise.

Your main goal is moving!

Get some free weights. It's all you need to start a strength-training regimen.

WHAT'S THE DIFFERENCE BETWEEN SHAMPOOS?

You don't need to spend a lot on shampoos. They're basically the same. If you want very clean hair, then look for the ingredient lauryl sulfate listed after water. If you have very fine hair or you wash your hair a lot, then just add a little water to your shampoo. Or use a little less shampoo. Experiment with quantities and you'll get the technique down pat.

Use a little SHAMPOO in your bath for a tub full of bubbles.

BANG YOUR BUCK

- Mix your regular foundation with a pale, shimmery eye shadow like gold or beige. This is a good substitute for a very expensive shimmery foundation.
- Always check the return policy of anything you're not absolutely sure about. Some stores offer full refunds even on opened or used products.

- Look at ethnic skin lines if you need more pigment from your products since they tend to be more intense.
- Dab a little antacid like Maalox on a pimple or cold sore.

FREE SAMPLES JUST FOR THE ASKING

Most cosmetic counters provide generous samples of skin care products, fragrances, and great little travel items like small tubes of lipstick. It's not something that is advertised, and counter people don't offer unless you ask.

Rather than just ask at each counter for anything free, pick a category. Ask about a fragrance you've seen. Look through the latest magazines. It's usually the newest products that have samples for customers to try.

- Try not to go when it's very busy.
- Don't ask, "What do you have for free?"
- Don't be greedy.
- Act like you really are interested. After all, you might really like that new fragrance.

CHEAP TRICKS

Use a creamy
BATHROOM CLEANSER
that's slightly abrasive to clean your light-colored shoes and sneakers. Just put a few drops on a cotton rag and wipe away!

MAKE YOUR OWN SOAP

These make great gifts, and an easy project to do with friends.

Mix 1¾ cups of soap flakes (like Ivory Snow) with ¼ cup water.

Use food coloring to create different colors.

Pour into ice cube trays or candy molds and let dry.

FABRIC MARKERS

There are lots of fun ways to use fabric markers to customize your wardrobe.

Always be sure to allow at least twenty-four hours to dry.

Shirt
Take an inexpensive T-shirt, preferably new, and machine wash and dry it. Pin the edges to a piece of cardboard, flattening out wrinkles and creases. Draw a flower or a name or even your favorite slogan.

Handbag
Match the colors of a basic bag to an outfit.

Sneakers
Customize your sneakers and make a statement that's totally you.

Jeans
Add life to an old pair of jeans with symbols and words.

FABRIC TRICKS

- Use a glue stick to edge hems and pockets of lace to a pair of cut off jeans.

- Dress up a boring T-shirt by trimming the neckline and sleeves.

- Hide a permanent stain with an inexpensive appliqué.

NO BELT? NO PROBLEM!

Use a scarf in contrasting or matching colors. Take a necklace and link it through the loops.

SCENT YOUR DRAWERS

Make your own sachets. You'll love the way your sweaters, lingerie, and hosiery smells when you open your drawers. Plus, these make thoughtful, inexpensive gifts.

You'll need:

2 pieces of fabric, about 5" x 5"

Lavender beads, rose petals, or pine needles

Needle and thread

Sew three sides of the fabric inside out.

Turn the fabric right side out.

Add just enough filling so that you can sew the final side.

You can sew by hand or machine.

MAKE A BATH SACHET

Fill knee-high nylon hose or the foot of panty hose with oatmeal, loose chamomile tea, or orange/lemon peel. Close the top with ribbon or just knot it. Tie it to the faucet under warm running water.

RECYCLE YOUR **TOOTHBRUSH** AND MAKE A COOL **BRACELET**

Pull the bristles of your toothbrush with tweezers.

Boil the brush in a saucepan anywhere from thirty minutes to up to two hours until softened.

Pull the toothbrush out with tongs and mold it around a bottle or glass.

Stick it in the freezer and wait until it hardens.

It's a great statement to put several colors on one arm.

BE YOUR OWN MAKEUP ARTIST

You don't need dozens of lipstick shades. Instead of buying, and buying, and buying, do what the most famous makeup artists do—mix your own colors together. Not only will you get your perfect shade, but you'll also save a ton of money.

USE A BRUSH TO DIP INTO THE TUBE.

Mix on wax paper until you get the color you like.

Chapter 7

STYLING

WHAT IS IT?

What we wear tells everyone who sees us who we are, or who we want them to think we are. Our style is our hope of who we will become. It helps us play a part. It makes us accepted, and it means that we accept ourselves.

Your style must be your own, not someone else's. So, how do you develop style? First you have to think about how you feel most comfortable. Jeans and T-shirt? All glam all the time? Classic casual? Each piece of clothing, each color shadow, and every piece of jewelry you wear again and again creates style.

But style is not just about clothing, makeup, jewelry, and hair. The attitude with which you present yourself is even more important. You need to feel comfortable and confident with your choices. A put-together attitude is what will stay with you and keep your style up-to-date.

WHY BOTHER?

It's simple. When you look your best, you'll feel even better.

IT'S A JOURNEY

When you do find something that looks great, feels great, and turns heads...buy two. Or three if you can afford it.

FIND YOUR LOOK, AND THEN WORK IT

The great thing about style is that it's up to you to determine what you like. You decide what your look will be, then add accessories to carry that look into different situations. You love white blouses? Dress them up with accessories. Wear them down with jeans.

PICK UP STYLE WHERE YOU CAN

It can come from a book, a movie, a thought.

WEARING THE TRENDS

Style goes beyond trends. It is something that you like, and you won't stop liking it just because someone says it's out.

SCHOOL GIRL

Mix preppie with a little bit of rocker.

Wear a logo tee with a sweater jacket.

Take a classic look and add funky sandals.

Don't take the cute look from head to toe. That's not cute, and you'll look like you're trying too hard.

Don't wear an outfit that's so totally matched it looks like a uniform.

MILITARY

One of two camouflage prints is enough.

Military pants call for a simple tee.

A camouflage top needs a simple pant or a metal belt. That's it!

Don't wear army boots with anything else that's military inspired.

Anything from the surplus store that is over-sized needs to be balanced with something close to the body.

EVERYDAY STYLE

Keep your wardrobe lean and mean. If you don't stuff your closet you can find what you need quickly. Plus, you won't have to struggle with your style on a daily basis.

Since we only wear a small portion of our wardrobe, you need background pieces in your closet. Keep style in your wardrobe with classic pieces and throw in a few trends when you can.

STAY **NEUTRAL**

Build your basic wardrobe in shades that go with a lot of other shades like black, navy, and brown. Then you can throw in the trendy colors of the season. There is a fine line between being stylish and being ridiculous.

MONEY PROBLEMS

The more you keep a simple shape, the more expensive your piece is going to look. Add to your simple piece with accessories. This is how you create your own style.

NEVER BE LATE FOR SCHOOL AGAIN!
Forget tons of jewelry or a hard-to-fix hairstyle. Add on only as much as you have time for.

JEANS STYLE

Life is a little easier once you find the perfect jeans. It's the basic bones on which you can develop a lot of looks. But finding the right jeans may mean trying on ten or twenty pairs.

CHECK THE **ZIPPER**

The zipper should be strong and lie flat. The flap over the zipper should also lie flat. The same rule applies to button style.

TUCK SOMETHING

If you can't tuck in your sweater, or at least a shirt, you need a bigger size.

CHECK THE **SEAMS**

They should run straight down your legs. This indicates a good fit. If a jean has any curve to it, it's either not the right cut for you, or it's too small.

BEND OVER

If you can't touch your palms to the ground, or you can't kneel, then your jeans won't be comfortable.

CHECK THE **WEIGHT**

The heavier the denim the more wear you'll get. It will be more forgiving to flaws.

CUFF OR **CUT**?

Cuffs are cute on slim jeans, and usually work better on longer legs. The cut, ragged look looks best with wide legs.

MIX IT UP

You can mix and match denim colors, but stick to one color palette. Light blue denim looks great with darker denim, but don't wear dark denim with black.

DRESS **UP**/DRESS **DOWN**

You can wear identical jeans in different ways. You can hem or cut one pair to wear with flats or clogs. Get an additional pair and wear them with chunky heels or boots.

HAVE **ONE OUTFIT** THAT YOU KNOW WORKS

Just one outfit a season can become your back-up...your time-saver. It is what you'll wear when you get that last-minute invitation. Don't ever refuse an invitation because you have nothing to wear.

JEANS CAMOUFLAGE

Pick slightly relaxed dark denim jeans. If there are pockets on the jean, they should be close-set.

Don't wear your jeans too tight, or with too much stretch to them.

MINI RULES

- Minis are hot for teens, but there's a fine line between trendy and tacky.
- Sit down and make sure you're not showing anything that you shouldn't.
- Wear tights for extra coverage.
- Don't ever wear nude hose. Use self-tanner instead.
- Stay away from minis in clingy fabrics or loose styles. They tend to ride up.
- Kilts and pleats are for cheerleaders.
- Knee-high boots always work.

WHITE TEES

- Cut corners by buying basic T-shirts from mass merchandise stores.
- If you're petite, save money in the boy's department.
- Look for styles that hug the body.
- Look for 35 to 40 percent polyester for easy care.
- Don't bother with the thick tees; they're for working out.
- The sleeves should be short, cutting right below the shoulder.

DRESSING SLIM

DARK BOTTOMS AND SHOES PROVIDE A LONG LINE. BULKY FABRICS BULK UP THE BODY.

GOING SHEER

Match your lingerie colors to the sheer garment.
Never wear sheer head to toe.
Sheers should never cling.
Don't reveal anything under sheer that you shouldn't.
Wear sheer as a camisole (under a cardigan or shirt) during the day.

LOOKING POLISHED

It's a fine line between looking grown up and looking like you're playing dress up.

Some girls just have the touch, the ability to give their outfits that special something without looking like they tried at all.

It's hard at first, especially if you've been used to casual dressing. You wonder how you're going to look pulled together like those celebrities, like those models in the magazine layouts.

You want to look like you, but more put together. Plus, you don't want to look like you tried too hard.

IT ALL STARTS WITH A DRESS

You're not too young to have a "go anywhere" dress. It's something that you can wear to your cousin's wedding, or on Easter Sunday. You can also dress it down with a big belt.

DON'T BE A SNOB

You don't have to spend a lot to look great, and you don't have to spend a lot of time on your looks to be pulled together.

YOU NEED A WATCH

The right watch can add class to any outfit. So now is the time to get rid of the big neo number. Plus, you need to keep track of time to make important time for beauty.

The good news is that you don't have to spend a lot on this accessory. There are many inexpensive knockoffs that look just like the real thing.

STYLE RULES

Don't save your best clothes for special events. Wear them when you want to and just because you feel like it. You be surprised how special a day can become.

Always dress to shop. This way, you're already styling before you walk into the store, and you won't be tempted because everything you try on looks better than what you have.

HAVE A SIGNATURE THAT YOU BECOME KNOWN FOR

Make it a scent, a color, or your love for flea markets that you also happen to wear.

It will make you feel special. It will make you memorable. Anyone who is known for their style has something that sets them apart from the pack.

BREAK IT UP

Polished does not mean that everything matches. You may be tempted to wear things that go together. Sometimes that's just not interesting, and you could look like you are trying too hard. Just because it comes together doesn't mean it always has to go together.

MESS IT UP

There's a way to look polished and casual at the same time. Play with your clothing. Push up the sleeves, take off the belt, or wear a suit jacket with jeans.

TAKE A CHANCE

Try something new in little doses. If you want to try an animal print, do an animal print belt, not pants. If you crave more, get more, little by little.

KEEP THINKING

Think about using things that you own in different ways. For instance, if you want to dress up a pair of jeans, use a necklace as a belt. Look at the things that you have in your closet and find new ways to use them.

Break Rules

FINGERNAILS & **TOENAILS** DON'T HAVE TO MATCH AND NEITHER DO YOUR CLOTHES.

YOU DON'T ALWAYS NEED JEWELRY. YOU ESPECIALLY DON'T NEED TO WEAR EVERY PIECE OF JEWELRY YOU OWN AT THE SAME TIME.

GOLD & **SILVER** CAN BE WORN TOGETHER.

LOSE IT

Be really strict with yourself. If it's over, it's over. Say good-bye either by removing it from your closet or giving it away.

GET GLAM YOUR OWN WAY

If you are more comfortable in a dress than pants, then that' s your style. When the occasion calls for a more casual look, then wear a long skirt and a tee.

BECOME HARD & SOFT

Wear something oh-my-goodness feminine with something masculine.

Chapter 8

DETAILS

THOSE FINISHING TOUCHES

It's what separates the stylish from those with a "style wish." It's a way to express your individuality, to update without spending a lot, and it completes a look. Important details include everything from underwear to your handbags.

You don't have to buy a lot to keep your style continually fresh. Instead, simply update your look with the accessory of the moment.

It's the finishing touch, that final little extra that pronounces your dose of style.

The wrong accessory also can ruin an otherwise great look. It can happen when you wear a huge shoulder bag with a gown.

THE PERFECT HANDBAG

It's such an important accessory, and so often overlooked. It's more visible than your shoes because it's right at eye level for everybody to notice.

You don't need a bag that's more than 10 x 13 inches unless it's for school books or travel.

It's not that important or necessary to match every outfit with an exactly matched bag. Actually it makes you look like you're trying too hard. Pick a neutral color or a multicolored bag if you want it to look like it goes with what you're wearing.

Find one with extra compartments to help you find things.

A small bag with a short shoulder strap will slim your hips and butt.

If you want to look less top heavy, let your bag fall at your waist or just below.

Look taller by locating a bag with a contrasting vertical detail.

Choose a bag that falls at the area that you consider your biggest asset, because that's where you'll be noticed.

⭐ EXTRA CREDIT: **LIGHTEN UP**

It's not necessary to carry everything in your purse, and it's not practical to carry full-sized products. Don't ever have a bag so big that people ask you what you could possibly have in there.

BASIC NEEDS

> Wallet
>
> Keys
>
> Breath mints
>
> Comb/brush
>
> Nail file
>
> Tissues
>
> Notebook and pen

Plus, a cosmetics bag with these essentials:

> Lipstick (doubles as blush)
>
> Foundation/powder combo
>
> Dual pencil for eyes, lips, brows

Don't try to carry loose powder in your purse unless it's in a separate container. It just makes a mess.

⭐ EXTRA CREDIT: **IF THERE'S ROOM**

> **Mascara**
>
> **Sewing kit with small scissors**
>
> **Baby wipes for face refreshing and removing stains**

STORE YOUR COSMETICS

in a clear pencil case. In this way, you can see everything at a glance without having to dig. Keep a mirror in it, facing outward. Not only will you protect the mirror from getting dirty, but you'll also be able to see yourself at a glance.

BACKPACKS

Backpacks are a great convenience both for school and hands-free shopping.
Make sure the backpack fits properly.

- It should have well-padded shoulder straps.
- Look for heavy stitching for strength.
- Consider one with retractable wheels for heavy loads.
- Look for compartments that are appropriate to your needs.

WISE WALLETS

- Consider a wallet's material first. Nylon is durable, easy to keep clean, and inexpensive.
- Leather gets better as it ages. Calfskin is the best leather for wallets.
- Light colors stain in any material.
- A leather change area is strongest.
- Edges should be finished, not frayed.

- Check for loose threads.
- Test to make sure the metal tops of the wallet "kiss."
- Test a zipper by tugging on the outside edges. Make sure it's strong and stays on track.

SHOES

Not only are they an important accessory, they can create an entire look. Let's face it. The shoes stage the outfit.

GO FOR COMFORT

If you can't wear a pair of shoes comfortably for more than an hour, don't bother. Your face will show your pain, no matter how much makeup you apply.

- There should be enough width to wiggle your toes.
- The end of your longest toe should be about ¼" to 1" from the end when you're standing.
- The widest part of the shoe should fit the widest part of your foot comfortably.

- The shoe should not slip when you walk.
- Buy late in the day when your feet are largest.
- Never buy a shoe that wrinkles when you flex your foot.

 **EXTRA CREDIT**
Wear What You Love
The shoes will dictate what follows.

FLATS LOOK BEST WITH LONG SKIRTS & SLIM PANTS.

SANDAL SOLUTIONS

The simpler the sandal, the more use you'll get.

Be sure the straps are well made, not too tight or too delicate.

Avoid sandals that cut any area of the foot.

Look for built-in arch support. Inner padding is the sign of a well-made sandal.

BOOT BOOSTERS

Chunky boots need heavier hose. Don't wear with sheer hose.

Buy your size. Boots should be snug without cramping. Don't buy boots that are too big.

Don't stuff your calves into the boot. Look for stretch materials if you have large calves.

Get non-skid soles from your shoemaker if your boots don't already have them.

EYEGLASSES

Here's a great way to show off your style. Your glasses can make your entire look a major statement.

A long narrow face looks best in oval frames. Cat's eye frames add width at the cheekbones.

Heart-shaped faces look best in oval or square frames, which hide width and create balance.

A round face is most flattered by an angled or squared shape since they add contours.

Soften a square face with round or oval frames. They help de-emphasize a strong jaw line.

Shorten a long nose with light wire frames.

Aviator styles help slim a broad face.

HAIR

Gold rims bring out golden highlights. Red or wine frames look great on redheads.

EYES

Tortoise shell is a good choice for brown eyes. Blue eyes sparkle in clear or silver frames.

JEWELRY

The quickest way you can change your look is with jewelry. It's like a punctuation mark at the end of a sentence. The very same dress can become dressy with crystal jewelry, or go casual with wooden accessories.

EARRINGS

You can actually change the shape of your face with the right pair of earrings.

Larger earrings make the nose look smaller.

Avoid drop or shoulder earrings if you have a long face or short neck.

Colored stones can brighten your complexion.

Big earrings look great on girls with larger faces.

Petite girls need delicate earrings.

Dangling earrings look best on short hair or with up-dos.

Smaller earrings look best with glasses.

WEAR ONLY ENOUGH JEWELRY TO COMPLEMENT YOUR OUTFIT, NOT OVERWHELM IT.

BELTS

The right belt can make you appear slimmer and taller. It can dress an outfit up or down.

A skinny belt can make your legs look longer. It draws the eye up, making your lower half look longer.

A thick middle can look smaller with a wide belt worn just below the waist. Wear it loosely.

Add height with a chain belt. Wear it loosely on your hips.

IF YOU WEAR A **WIDE BELT**, LET IT REST ON YOUR HIPS. WEARING IT RIGHT AT THE WAIST WILL MAKE THE BELT LOOK LIKE A CORSET.

HATS

They're a great accessory, but not for everyone. They look best when worn outdoors.

Once you have a hat on, you need to keep it on. Hat head is a sure thing.

SUNGLASSES

A great accessory, but you've got to look at more than the style.

- Plastic frames are less likely to pop out but scratch easily.
- Polarized lenses filter out glare.
- Mirrored lenses reflect it back.
- Green works well in low and bright light.
- Brown and amber are good for high glare or haze.
- Gray, rose, and yellow are good for outdoor sports.

Bag Fun

DECORATE AN INEXPENSIVE LUNCHBOX FOR A FUN BAG.

Cut pictures from magazines, use pictures of friends, your family, anything that **MAKES A STATEMENT**.

Arrange them on the **LUNCHBOX** using double-stick tape.

Once you get the look you want, **PASTE THE PICTURES** on with nontoxic glue.

Then just **SPRAY** over everything with a clear shellac.

Chapter 9

NATURAL LOOKS

Staying natural is a simple way to enjoy your beauty and at the same time key in to your inner beauty. It means you're taking care of yourself because you care about yourself. It also means that you're in touch with your environment.

The good news is that the all-natural look can be achieved by yourself, and with inexpensive items you already may have around the house.

NATURAL SKIN

NATURAL ACNE TREATMENTS

High-fiber cereals

Have one bowl a day to control inflammation of the skin.
Check the side of the box for the fiber content. Look for cereals that have at least five grams.

Zinc

Include it in your diet or check with your doctor to see if you should take a zinc supplement.

Blemish-Busting Mask

Mix ½ teaspoon turmeric with enough water to form a paste. Apply to blemishes and leave on overnight.

You'll find turmeric in the baking aisle of your local supermarket.

SOOTHE INFLAMED SKIN WITH **WITCH HAZEL.**

Honey/Orange Five-Minute Mask

Apply ½ cup honey with ½ cup orange juice to blemishes. Leave on five minutes before rinsing. The honey contains hydrogen peroxide, which inhibits bacteria, while the citric acid in the juice will dry up excess oil.

A little **TEA TREE OIL** mixed with an equal amount of warm water can be used to wash acne-prone areas.

Blackhead Remover

Here's a way to get rid of blackheads naturally (and without squeezing!).

Dissolve one tablespoon unflavored gelatin in two tablespoons milk over low heat.

Let cool and apply to face.

Leave on thirty minutes.

As you peel off the mask, you'll peel off the blackheads.

NATURAL WAYS TO EXFOLIATE (REMOVE THE TOP LAYER OF DIRT AND DEBRIS)

Powdered milk with water is a clean and natural milk cleanser. Plus, it's convenient since you don't have to refrigerate it.

Salt is good for chafed skin or for getting a peeling sunburn off. Mix ½ teaspoon salt with a teaspoon of water.

Baking soda with water is a good wash for very sensitive skin. Put a little baking soda in the palm of your hand, and then add just enough water to make a paste.

INSTANT SKIN-REVIVER

Squeeze an orange and pat the liquid on your face with your fingers. The citrus liquid and scent will evaporate quickly, but you'll look awesome. It's all thanks to the vitamin C, an antioxidant that gives a great glow.

CHEAP & EFFECTIVE

Moisturize your body with a vegetable shortening like Crisco. Moisturize your face only if it's extremely dry or sunburned.

Avocado Face Mask

Mash a teaspoon of ripe avocado with ½ teaspoon lemon juice.

Massage into face and neck.

Let dry, and then rinse off with cool water.

Orange Peel

This peel will restore skin tone and even out sunburn. Combine one peeled, chopped orange with two tablespoons of coarse sea salt. Massage mixture on dry skin and let sit for five minutes. Rinse well.

NATURAL BODY SOLUTIONS

- Check the refrigerator and grab up all the old, overripe oranges, lemons, and grapefruit you can find. Cut them up and put them in your bath. Keep it clean by putting the fruit into the foot of old panty hose and tying it on the faucet so that the water flows through the fruit. It will make your skin smooth and silky, plus you'll love the real citrus scent.
- Add some great moisture and scent to your bath with almond oil or apricot kernel.
- Before bathing or showering, chop and mash an apple. Then stir in a cup of sugar. Rub the mixture all over your body, concentrating on the dry areas like your elbows and heels.
- After shaving, treat razor burns with an inexpensive wet tea bag. The cheaper the tea, the more tannic acid it has, which will reduce redness.
- Treat your bikini line with olive oil. It's full of vitamin E and will help prevent ingrown hairs.
- Sprinkle one cup uncooked oatmeal in your tub to soak away dry, itchy skin.

One Ingredient Masks

Spread an egg white all over clean skin and let dry. Rinse thoroughly.

✳

Spread plain yogurt over the face to even out skin tone. Leave on 5 minutes and rinse.

✳

Mash ½ a ripe peach and spread on face to bring out the glow. Leave on 10 to 15 minutes.

✳

Crush a tomato (peel it first) and spread it over your face. Tomatoes contain acids
that balance the skin's pH levels and tighten pores. Leave on 10 minutes and rinse thoroughly.

✳

Mash half a banana and rub it into clean, dry skin. Leave on for five minutes.
Then rinse well. This mask will leave your skin baby soft, plus the potassium in
the banana will help erase any undereye circles.

✳

Mash two strawberries and spread them over clean, dry skin. Leave on for five minutes.
The strawberries erase blemishes because they're high in salicylic acid, the active ingredient
in most over-the-counter acne treatments. The strawberry seeds will slough off rough
patches caused by blemishes for instantly smoother skin.

107

NATURAL BEAUTY RECIPES

ROSE BODY POLISH

Go into the garden and pick a few roses

Combine ½ cup Epsom salts with scented shower or bath gel to make a paste.

Stir in a handful of fresh crushed roses.

Rub into damp skin.

MILK BATH TREAT

Mix two cups dry whole-milk powder with one cup cornstarch.

Add one teaspoon of almond or vanilla extract.

Stir together in a pretty container, and leave by the tub.

Pour about ½ cup into running bath water to smooth and soften skin.

SKIN BUFFER

Blend two cups crushed macadamia nuts with two sprigs of fresh mint, ½ cup of honey and ½ teaspoon almond extract.

Mix it all into a paste.

Rub all over your body.

Rinse and pat skin dry.

COMPLEXION CORRECTING FACIAL

Step 1

One teaspoon honey

One egg white

Mix together and apply to face.

Allow to dry and rinse.

Step 2

Mash one banana with a tablespoon of avocado. Leave on for ten minutes and rinse.

The banana is full of vitamin B to nourish your skin, while the egg white will absorb oil.

CUCUMBER PARSLEY TONER

This will keep your skin balanced and refreshed. Mix one cup warm water with two tablespoons chopped parsley, ½ russet potato (scrubbed but not peeled), ¼ unpeeled cucumber, one teaspoon almond extract, and two teaspoons lemon juice in a pan. Bring to a boil. Remove from heat and cool.

Apply to skin with a cotton swab.

SKIN POLISH

Buff skin in the shower with a little brown sugar mixed with some vanilla extract.

Rinse and then pat your skin (don't rub) with a thick towel.

Use your favorite body lotion mixed with another drop of vanilla extract.

PEACH SMOOTHIE

Peel and mash a ripe peach. Strain to extract all of the juice.

Mix juice with an equal amount of heavy whipping cream.

Massage into skin and leave on about fifteen minutes.

Rinse with warm water.

The gentle fruit acid from the peach and the lactic acid from the cream will soothe and smooth your skin.

SUNBURN-RELIEVER

Mix one teaspoon aloe vera gel with one teaspoon honey. Apply it to the affected area for a few minutes. Then rinse with cool water. This mixture will cool the skin while preventing peeling.

ATHLETE'S FOOT RELIEF

Mix one tablespoon baking soda and ¼ cup water.

Rub between toes to relieve the itch of athlete's foot.

Leave mixture on until it dries.

Rinse and dry feet completely.

NATURAL HAIR TREATS

MEDITERRANEAN HAIR MASK

Massage a teaspoon of olive oil into the scalp for about two to three minutes.

Then brush through the hair.

Wrap it in a towel for thirty minutes and then shampoo.

SUN STREAKS

Before heading outside, slick your hair into a ponytail coated with leave-in conditioner.

Then coat lightly over the entire head. You'll be amazed at how absolutely sun-kissed your hair looks after thirty minutes of "sun" treatment.

MAKE SOME WAVES

After swimming in the ocean, make a braid or several braids in your hair. When your hair dries, take them out for gorgeous waves.

SCALP MASSAGE

This is just like a very expensive scalp massage models love!

Soak a towel in a bowl of hot water and five cucumber and five lemon slices.

Wring the towel, and wrap it around your head.

Relax and breathe deeply for about ten minutes.

Remove towel.

In the palm of your hand mix a few drops of tea tree oil with a few drops of jojoba oil.

Massage your scalp, making circles with your fingers.

Shampoo thoroughly.

HAIR SALADS

Mix one tablespoon apple cider vinegar into a quart of water and rinse your hair with it when you shower. The vinegar helps to eliminate flaking.

Mix two tablespoons fresh lemon juice with two tablespoons apple cider vinegar and one tablespoon mayonnaise. Slather on dry hair (concentrate on the ends). Leave on for twenty minutes.

Rinse with very warm water.

DEEP CLEANSING SHAMPOO

Mix the contents of a green-tea bag and two tablespoons of olive oil, with the juice of a half a lemon and half an orange. Whip in a blender. Then massage into hair and leave on for fifteen minutes. Shampoo and condition.

HAIR REVIVER

Mash a ripe mango with one tablespoon of plain yogurt. Add two egg yolks.

Blend and spread all over hair. Cover with plastic wrap or a shower cap and leave on for about twenty minutes. Shampoo out thoroughly.

OREGANO & VANILLA HAIR DETANGLER

Mix ½ cup fresh oregano leaves or 2 teaspoons dried oregano, one teaspoon vanilla extract, and one cup water.

Microwave for thirty to forty seconds. When cool, strain and pour into a spray bottle. Use after shampooing and conditioning. Leave in refrigerator for up to seven days.

SHINE-BOOSTING CONDITIONER

Brew a cup of tea in a flavor close to your hair color.

Blonde/Chamomile

Brunette/black currant

Redhead/Orange pekoe

Mix equal parts tea with hair conditioner.
Use once or twice a week.

ADD HAIR VOLUME

Steep a bag of nettle tea in a cup of water and apply to clean and conditioned hair while damp. Nettle coats and thickens your hair shaft.

111

DANDRUFF TREATMENT

Boil 2 tablespoons of dried thyme in a cup of water. Cool, strain, and pour on your scalp. Don't rinse out. Thyme has antiseptic properties.

NATURALLY BEAUTIFUL HANDS AND FEET

NAILS

Rub jojoba oil or almond oil on your cuticles and fingers to keep them healthy and to stop them from splitting.

Get your nails white by dipping them in half a lemon for a minute or two.

The citric acid naturally bleaches tips.

THE POWERFUL PINEAPPLE

It's a great fruit with citric qualities that many spas use.

PINEAPPLE CUTICLE TREATMENT

Use this treatment before pushing back your cuticles.

¼ cup pineapple

½ teaspoon apple cider vinegar

One teaspoon vegetable oil

One tablespoon honey

One egg yolk

Mix together and apply to hands, concentrating on cuticles. Wrap hands in plastic gloves or plastic wrap. Leave on for fifteen minutes. Remove plastic and rinse with warm water.

PINEAPPLE FOOT SMOOTHER

Use once or twice a week to keep your feet sandal-ready!

½ cup chopped pineapple

½ unpeeled apple

½ lemon (peeled)

¼ grapefruit (peeled)

Two teaspoons anise extract

One teaspoon salt

Mix ingredients together. Rub mixture on feet, concentrating on heels. Wrap feet in plastic and leave on for twenty to thirty minutes. Rinse with warm water.

HAND/ARM THERAPY

There's a wonderful (but expensive) Tahitian scrub sold at spas that you can make yourself for under a dollar.

Grind ½ cup shelled walnuts into a powder

Add two tablespoons olive oil and one tablespoon of honey.

Rub over hands and lower arms for a few minutes.

Rinse well.

GET RID OF WARTS

Birch bark tea is the secret way that models get rid of warts without surgery or prescriptions. Boil the tea bag in a small amount of water, and let it cool.

Break it open and rub it on the wart daily until it disappears.

NATURAL MAKEUP

Natural beauty doesn't mean you won't ever wear makeup. You can wear lipstick, eyeliner, and even foundation and still look both natural and fresh-faced.

NATURAL FACE

Highlight, don't hide your natural skin tone. Rather than foundation, give your face a natural flush by combining moisturizer with foundation or self-tanner and lightly dotting your face.

Natural Pedicure

- Toss 5 bags of green tea into a basin of hot water. Let cool until comfortable and put both feet and ankles in.

- Let soak until water cools completely.

- Rub fresh mint leaves over your toes and feet.

- Apply olive oil to seal in moisture.

If you do wear foundation, it should go just where you need it. Completely matte skin looks unnatural and old-fashioned. Apply it with your fingers so that it will spread more easily.

ALL DAY LIPS

Jell-O is the big makeup artist secret for staining lips for all day. Wet your finger, dip it into the crystals (they quickly dissolve), and then rub it on your lips. Make the look even sweeter with lip gloss.

NATURALLY BEAUTIFUL LASHES

Drizzle a bit of olive oil on a toothbrush or lash comb and gently comb lashes for a darker, glossy look.

The **REAL SECRET** to achieving a natural look is to blend everything.

YOUR LIPSTICK WITH YOUR LINER.

YOUR FOUNDATION & CHEEK BLUSH.

YOUR EYE SHADOW & EYELINER.

STICK WITH ONE COLOR

It looks more natural to stay within the same color range. Stick to just one hue. Needless to say, pink lips, green eye shadow, and red blush is anything but natural looking.

DON'T FIGHT IT!

Work with what you've been given. It requires a lot of time and looks too precise to try to alter the shape of your lips or eyes. There's no way you'll achieve that natural look.

OPEN YOUR EYES

Didn't get enough sleep? Not feeling so well? Rest a bag of frozen peas on your eyes for ten minutes. Peas form to the shape of your brow, so other frozen vegetables won't work. ✶ Brighten your eyes by framing them with eyeliner in the color of the outer rim of your iris. ✶ Line lips with a pencil that matches your natural lip color.

ESSENTIAL OILS

Here are some essential oils that no natural beauty should be without!

LAVENDER

Helps with burns, sprains, healing wounds, and calming the mind and body.

Use it on your pillow, or dab it around your room when you want to relax.

Add a couple of drops to your bath.

EUCALYPTUS

Aids in clearing up skin infections and is a natural insect repellent. Put some inside your pillow to help you breathe more easily, especially if you have a cold.

Add a couple of leaves to boiling water to steam your face.

TEA TREE OIL

Helps cold sores, oily skin, athlete's foot, and blemishes. Use it straight from the bottle.

GERANIUM

Helps fade broken capillaries. Use it at night to heal bruises.

GRAPEFRUIT

Tones skin and tissues and helps with bloating. You'll love it as a bath oil. Use about ten drops under running water.

PEPPERMINT

It soothes digestion and is cool and refreshing. Apply it in the air or on the skin.

ALWAYS BE CAREFUL, WHEN APPLYING ANY ESSENTIAL OIL TO SKIN, ESPECIALLY SENSITIVE SKIN. TEST IT FIRST.

Chapter 10

MAKING SENSE

THE MIND/BODY CONNECTION

You've heard about inner beauty being as important (if not more) than outer beauty.

It only makes sense that if you're having a beauty crisis, it often can be solved from within. With a few tools and a little common sense you can be solving your problems in a matter of moments.

IT'S OK TO LOOK OUT FOR #1

It's not selfish, it's only self-survival. This is the time of your life when you are learning to take care of yourself. No matter how busy you are in a day, make time to do at least one thing that makes you feel or look better.

BAD HABITS

Keep a reminder of the benefit of making the change. Give yourself an extra incentive. For example, keep in mind the perfect jewelry you'll buy once you stop biting your nails.

BELIEVE IN YOUR INTUITION

It's not a big voice, but a feeling that will lead you into the direction you should go.

MAKE DECISIONS

Don't waste time sitting on the fence. Should you cut your hair or not? Decide and keep going. Don't let it stop you from moving on and growing stronger.

LABELS ARE FOR CLOTHING

They don't belong on people. You know the ones: "the pretty one," "the stupid one," "the chubby one," "the funny one," etc. These labels can follow you through your life. Don't accept a label, or wear one. There are many parts of a person.

SHE DOESN'T MEAN YOU!

WHEN A PARENT DISPARAGES HER OWN THIGHS OR STATES OUT LOUD THAT SHE WILL NEVER AGAIN WEAR A BATHING SUIT UNLESS THIRTY POUNDS DISAPPEAR, REMEMBER THAT YOU'RE NOT YOUR MOTHER.

Don't buy into your mother's flaws.

GET YOUR REST

Beauty is as beauty does. Just as those partying, drug-taking models don't keep their looks, you won't either if you don't get your beauty zzzz's.

- Keep regular sleep hours. Develop a routine.
- Relax in a bath or shower for at least thirty minutes so you can really feel the benefits.
- Start your ritual about an hour before bedtime.

DON'T WORRY OVER MONEY

Even if you can't afford weekly shopping binges, that's not a reason not to look fabulous.

It's not important what you spend, but how you spend, and how you put things together.

Some of the most fashionable models get their style by wearing vintage and thrift shop finds. And they love the thrill of the hunt.

WHAT IF

What if you weren't shy? Act for a moment like that. Take a deep breath and talk to yourself. Picture yourself speaking with confidence, and go for it.

Before heading out the door, write down everything that you're anxious about.

"What if nobody talks to me?"

Well, you should have something interesting to say, and talk to them. Say something nice, that's always a great icebreaker. Admire something they're wearing or their hairstyle.

"What if people laugh at me?"

What could you possibly do that would make that happen?

Get my point? You'll begin to see that all your anxiety is unwarranted.

RESPECT YOURSELF

Don't put anything in or on your body that will not benefit it in some way.

Don't deprive your body of nourishment.

Don't waste your time gossiping when you could be helping.

Be safe in who you let into your door and your life.

SENSE THE VIBES

You know if someone is really paying you a compliment. These feelings also will serve you well in picking out an outfit or choosing your friends. Trust it.

YOU CAN'T FOOL YOURSELF

Trying to reason with yourself is just too easy. You've got to train your rational inner voice to win over your less rational side.

"I'm too busy to eat. I'll just grab a candy bar."

Tell yourself that the world won't stop if you stop for fifteen minutes to eat a nutritious meal.

HOW MUCH IS ENOUGH?

Know how much shampoo to use. Directions will tell you to shampoo twice. That's rarely necessary. How much acne treatment do you really need? How about cleanser? Start with a dot and work up.

TAKE BABY STEPS

When it all seems just too overwhelming, take one step at a time. When I do a makeover, I ease the client into it. As much fun as those makeovers are to watch, most of them take days, but appear to take place in minutes. You need to make adjustments and tweaks as you go along. You are always a work in progress. Keep changing and you'll never be bored with life or yourself.

EXTRA CREDIT

Don't take on more than you can handle!

L E S S IS M O R E

There's a big difference between makeup and

wearing a clown face. Learn when to stop.

BROADEN YOUR PERSPECTIVE

You are not a size, a color, or a culture. They're all part of what makes you complete, but you should never be defined by them.

RECOGNIZE ROADBLOCKS

Don't let a remark, a pig-out, or a bad hair day ruin your perspective. A slip-up is never a failure. It's an opportunity to learn what works, what doesn't work, and what needs to be done differently.

WHAT'S THE REAL PROBLEM?

Maybe you're eating because you're tired. Then the common sense solution is to get more rest. Are you neglecting to wash your hair because you talked on the phone too long? Set a timer so you can have time for yourself.

Don't want to miss your favorite show and you need to work out? Tape it, and feel good about yourself while watching it later.

IT'S A TOTAL PACKAGE

Before you waste your money on a new shade of lipstick, realize that no matter how expensive, it will only look good if you take care of your lips. The same goes for clothes—that designer shirt should be hung properly and ironed to do it justice.

BE REALISTIC

Know that if you've never weighed 110 pounds in your life, your body is not meant to go there. Don't waste precious time trying to achieve unrealistic goals.

⭐ EXTRA CREDIT: **FRAME SIZE**

Find your frame size by taking your thumb and third finger and placing them around your opposite wrist. If they overlap, you have a small frame. If they just meet, you have a medium frame. If they don't touch, then you have a large frame. When you're checking out the charts, you'll see a twenty- to twenty-five–pound weight range depending on your frame.

CHECK YOURSELF

Knowing your body and its needs will keep you healthy and looking your very best. Here's a trick that models use to see if they need more water or moisturizer.

Pinch the skin on back of your hand. If the skin snaps back, then your body is properly hydrated. If it stays up for a few seconds, then drink more water and apply lotion to your body.

Your nails can indicate a whole crateful of problems. Splitting nails, white spots, slow growth, thickening, should be pointed out to your family doctor. Check the chapter on hands and feet for some beauty remedies.

ASK YOURSELF QUESTIONS

Solve your beauty dilemmas by writing down your question in the morning.

Then go through your day. At night, read your question again. You will most likely have a reasonable answer. Your best answers are inside of you.

USE ALL YOUR SENSES

When your mind is telling you to do something, but your tummy is doing cartwheels, then maybe it's not totally right.

AN OUNCE OF PREVENTION

It makes sense to prevent beauty and health problems as well as to solve them.

Always wash and dry your hands before touching your face.

Kill bacteria on your phone and doorknobs with rubbing alcohol or bleach.

PREVENT PIG OUTS

You can certainly use techniques to keep you from going over the edge when eating.

- Pay attention to portion sizes.
- Fill half your plate with greens.
- Eat out where a varied menu is offered. Even the most hip fast food joints now have healthy alternatives. You don't need to ruin your social life.

MAKE SOME SENSE

Here are lots of "why didn't I think of that" moments that will really make a difference.

Don't wear perfume when you'll be exposed to the sun. It will cause spot burning.

If you're going to be out all day, you'll need to reapply your sunscreen every couple of hours.

Don't cross your legs at the knees. It may look very ladylike, but it's putting an uneven amount of pressure on one hip and your back. Even more important, it will decrease circulation in your legs. Can anyone say "VEINS"?

Cover blemishes with a concealer, but make sure you seal in the concealer with a coating of powder.

Layer a matching shadow over your eyeliner to make the color last longer.

Keep your eyebrows from going all over the place by dabbing them with petroleum jelly or hairspray.

When wearing a bright lipstick, it's necessary to mute the rest of your face.

Switch to gloss at night for a dramatic effect.

Add sheen to your face with highlighting cream or go over your contours with a bit of baby oil.

Rub sunscreen over your nails to keep color from fading.

Use a deodorant soap when you exercise.

NO WAY!

Sometimes we hear something that doesn't make sense. If it sounds too good, or too easy...be careful.

• Don't take a pill or buy a cream thinking that it will increase your bust size.

• There is no eye cream out there that will immediately take away puffy eyes.

• Your skin care doesn't have to come from the same line so they can work with each other.

• Weight-loss pills are not necessary to lose weight.

NO-BRAINERS THAT DO WORK

Drink as much water as you can throughout the day. You'll feel better, look better, and have more energy.

Try to eat something in the morning. It takes little time, and the advantages are awesome. You won't have hunger pains in school, your energy level will stay up, and you'll be able to concentrate. Plus, your metabolism will be faster.

If you feel bloated, don't get on the scale. That number will only make you feel worse.

View exercise as something you do for yourself, rather than a punishment. It's a way you can be your very best—to go places you never thought you could.

Chapter 11

BODY CHALLENGES

Here's the good news. Nobody's perfect, and you certainly don't have to advertise your less-than-perfect body parts.

Create an optical illusion with lines.

Vertical lines add height.

Horizontal lines add width.

GET THE LOOK YOU WANT

SWEATERS

Trim your waist with a snug, belted, or wraparound cardigan that defines the waist.

Avoid oversized sweaters.

Get a flat tummy with a full-length sweater worn over a matching shell

Avoid body-hugging, lightweight fabrics.

Trim hips with a brightly colored sweater that ends just above the hip to balance.

Avoid sweaters that fall just at or below the hip.

Bring attention to the upper half of your body with interesting necklines that draw the attention there.

PANTS

For a flatter tummy, look for flat-front pants that have stitched down pleats and a bit of Lycra. Avoid pockets and open pleats.

For slimmer hips, go for wide-leg pants in lightweight fabrics. Avoid prints or side pockets.

For longer legs, choose pinstripes or slightly flared styles. Avoid cuffs or full legs.

For a smaller waist, look for boot-cut styles and a lowered waistband. Avoid baggy styles or high waists that end above the natural waistband.

PLUS SIZE TRICKS

• Don't wear oversized clothing

• Flaunt your curves by letting material skim, not stick.

• Use ¾ length to add length and streamline.

- Wear the proper undergarments. They should smooth out lines and support you.
- Stay away from straight lines.
- Bare what you like. The eye always goes first to the greatest exposure of skin.

OTHER SLIMMING TRICKS

One color head to toe.
Heels rather than flats.
Hose and shoes that match.
Belt and pants that match.

STAY AWAY FROM

Details where you don't want other eyes to stick.

Anything too tight—it just makes you look larger.

Large prints or plaids below the waist

Pleats that don't lie flat.

So much color that it draws attention away from your face.

Think of a **COLOR THAT MAKES YOU HAPPY.** That's the one to go for. Wearing different shades of the same color gives you height.

WHEN GOOD COLOR GOES WRONG

Large areas of light colors make figure flaws look bigger. Even black can be unflattering when it's shiny.

SHORTS FOR YOUR SHAPE

Disguise a tummy with flat-front shorts.

Large thighs can look slimmer with shorts that cover the thigh and end above the knee.

If you have short legs, wear shorts with vertical stripes.

SHOWING LESS TOP

If you want people to notice you, not your chest, rely on these tricks.

- Choose dark-colored, solid tops with high necklines. Dark colors take the emphasis away from the area.
- Stay away from low-cut, revealing necklines.
- Stay away from anything that doesn't require a bra.
- Skip stretchy fabrics.
- Keep jewelry at the neckline or above.

Chapter 12

FOOD FOR THOUGHT

Your feelings about food right now can make a huge impact on how you live the rest of your life.

YOUR GOOD HABITS WILL PAY OFF

By eating the right foods, your body will work better, your hair will shine, and your skin will behave. Plus you'll have a great feeling of being in control.

Get enough sleep. When you're tired, it's hard to make good decisions, especially about food.

Watch your portions. Just because you're given a certain portion at a restaurant or school doesn't mean that amount is what your body needs. Eat only until you're comfortably full. A little on your plate each day adds up to a long-term decrease in calories.

Don't ignore your sweet tooth. A hard candy is only about twenty calories and can last up to twenty minutes. A four hundred-calorie ice cream never lasts more than ten minutes.

Learn to spice it up. You'll get more flavor for your bite and more satisfaction.

Personalize your program. Eat what you like and explore new foods.

Eat during the day. Unless you do, you're more apt to overeat at night.

Eat breakfast. You're not saving calories, you're losing energy.

Act goofy. Even if you're too busy for the gym, you can still do cardio. Put on a pair of socks, and slide around the house like a skater. You'll burn 150 calories in just ten minutes.

Don't be too hard on yourself. If you have a diet plan that's too low for your weight and energy level, you'll slow down your metabolism as your body attempts to conserve calories. Don't dip below twelve hundred calories or more than a one- to two-pound weight loss a week.

Go for it. If you want a cookie, then have it. If you try to avoid your craving by having a slice of toast, it's not going to satisfy you.

FEED YOUR FACE

There's a saying in modeling that applies to how you should approach food:

"If you eat it, then you wear it." It's an old saying, but doesn't it make complete sense?

If it goes into your body, it becomes your body. Even with all the other good things that you do to your body, nothing is more important than what you put in it.

Rather than reaching for that jar of cream that you probably paid too much for, reach for something fresh and delicious to eat.

EATING DISORDERS

Don't ruin your life by trying to take shortcuts to weight loss. You will greatly regret it. The effects on your looks and health are never worth it.

BULIMIA

Usually binge eating followed by vomiting, laxative use, and exercise.

Girls who do this are usually average weight or even slightly overweight.

Vomiting won't rid the body of all the food.

WARNING SIGNS

Swollen glands

Running to the bathroom after eating

Scarred knuckles

Binge Eating

Compulsive overeating countered with days of fasting. Usually the binging is done in secret in a short amount of time.

Anorexia

Eating a minimum of food (sometimes no food) for days, weeks, even months.

WARNING SIGNS

Intense fear of gaining weight

Talking constantly about weight and size

Sudden weight loss

Cooks for others, but doesn't eat herself

Refuses to eat certain foods

GET HELP!

Most eating disorders require professional help. If left untreated, eating disorders can develop into severe health problems, even death.

Extreme vomiting upsets the body's balance of sodium, potassium, and other body essentials. Plus, you'll feel fatigued, and you may develop an irregular heartbeat and damage your bones. Some bulimics damage the enamel on their teeth so badly that they need to have their teeth pulled!

The great looks that many girls hope to achieve by starving and abusing themselves never happens, and instead they are left with skin rashes, broken blood vessels in the face, and irregular menstrual cycles. Other eating disorder effects can include dry skin, hair breakage, and brittle nails.

About one thousand women die of anorexia each year, according to the American Anorexia/Bulimia Association. The majority of these deaths happen to women between the ages of twelve and eighteen.

WHERE TO GO

Don't be afraid or ashamed to ask for help. If you can't talk to your parents, a doctor, or your school nurse, then get information as soon as possible. The earlier a disorder is treated, the less likely the damage will become permanent.

American Anorexia/Bulimia Association Inc.
239 Central Park West
Suite 1R
New York, NY 10024
212-501-8351

National Association of Anorexia and Associated Disorders
P.O. Box #7
Highland Park, IL 60035
847-831-3438

A Healthy Weight

JUST BECAUSE YOUR FRIEND WEIGHS 110 POUNDS DOESN'T MEAN THAT YOUR BODY IS MEANT TO WEIGH THE SAME. SHARE BEAUTY TIPS, NOT WEIGHT GOALS.

FRIENDS AND FOOD

Be a food leader, not a follower.

YOU CAN EAT PIZZA

Topped with veggies, a pizza is a great meal filled with nutrients. So when everyone else is ordering, just forget the pepperoni and sausages.

YOU CAN SNACK

You just have to plan ahead.

Snacks Less than 150 Calories

Two Oreo cookies

McDonald's ice cream cone

Half a cup of Italian ice

Starbucks Frappuccino ice cream bar

Jell-O with whipped cream

Fudgsicle

CHANGE YOUR WAYS

Just a few changes can make all the difference!

- Order thin crust pizza instead of thick.
- Make tuna with light mayo or switch to a veggie burger.
- Have a Happy Meal instead of a Big Mac.
- Top your baked potato with salsa in place of butter and sour cream.

NEVER miss an event just because you're on a diet. You should always go for the friends, never the food.

PARENTS AND OTHER RELATIVES

When I was modeling, I remember my grandmother insisting I eat an éclair, and I had a big job that required me to be a certain size. This darling woman was an example of so many well-meaning family members.

- A little of everything won't put on weight, it's those second and third helpings that will.
- Decline seconds. Tell that well-meaning relative

that you loved the food, but you are truly full.

- If you don't want to eat dessert, then choose fruit. Become the example for your family.

EATING ON THE ROAD

TRY TO KEEP A SCHEDULE

Eating at odd times can throw off your inner clock. You want to start now to set up body rhythms to work with your digestive tract. If you find this hard to do by yourself, start keeping a food journal. It will tell you when you're most hungry and need to eat.

MAKE A DIFFERENCE

Go for two stairs at a time instead of one. Speed walk to the school bus or mall.

CONCENTRATE

Keep food out of sight while you're:

- Watching TV
- Reading
- Studying
- Answering email

GET OUT

Try to spend twenty minutes a day sitting outside or taking a walk. If you can't, at least sit by a sunny window. Sunlight helps to control food cravings.

AT THE MALL

Order a mini meal.

A yogurt is a quick pick-me-up.

Have a salad without heavy dressings.

THE SKINNY ON RESTAURANTS

CHINESE

Order a stir-fried dish made with lean meat or fish instead of sweet and sour chicken or pork.

Have won ton soup instead of fried won tons.

Avoid foods with MSG.

Avoid buffets since the foods usually contain more oil to keep from drying out.

BARBECUE/ROTISSERIE

Take the skin off the chicken.

Order sirloin steak or chicken with dipping sauce on the side.

DELI/SUB SHOP

Go for the roast turkey or roast beef in place of tuna or chicken salad.

ITALIAN

Go for the pasta with meat sauce instead of cream.

Tortellini with spinach or meat is a good choice since it requires less sauce.

Order a side dish of pasta.

Instead of the bread, order some soup. It will fill you up without the extra calories.

MEXICAN

A bean burrito has fiber to keep you full for a longer period.

Corn tortillas have half the calories of flour tortillas.

Have your beans unfried.

Top everything with salsa.

FAST FOOD MENUS

You can eat anywhere as long as you make the right choices, even at fast food restaurants.

ARBY'S

Side salad/25 calories
Roast chicken salad/160 calories

BURGER KING

Broiled chicken salad/200 calories
Garden salad/25 calories (no dressing)

DAIRY QUEEN

Fudge bar/50 calories
Lemon freeze/no calories
DQ sandwich/200 calories

KFC

Mean greens/70 calories
Tender Roast Chicken Breast without skin (4 ounce serving)/170 calories
Red Beans and Rice/126 calories and 4 grams of fat.

MCDONALDS

Grilled Chicken Caesar Salad/100 calories
Garden salad/100 calories

PIZZA HUT

Thin & Crispy pizza (1 slice with ham) 190 calories

SUBWAY

Veggie Delite/226 calories

Avoid anything with the words "jumbo" or "biggie."

Stay away from CHEESE and MAYO and eat all you want of pickles, mustard, and ketchup.

Be careful with the toppings you choose. A perfectly healthy salad can add on calories with the **WRONG DRESSING**. Steer clear of sour cream, cheese, butter, and mayo.

ZERO in on the vegetarian items, which usually have the least calories.

TRICKS AND TECHNIQUES

ACUPRESSURE

Stay away from the pills and other money-eating gimmicks and try this technique to wake up your metabolism and speed digestion.

Put your hands in front of your tummy and clasp your hands, gently interlocking your fingers. With your palms touching your tummy, move your hands in clockwise circles.

Repeat fifty times.

Try something new, even those odd-looking **VEGGIES** on your family table.

CHANGE YOUR HABITS

Cut out your least loved calories, and eat what you love the most before anything else. So if you love pretzels, enjoy them. Maybe you can live without the chips.

Don't eat in response to feelings. You can't stuff them down with food

Don't eat unless you've made a place setting.

Give up one bad eating habit. For instance, eat in the kitchen, not in front of the TV or in bed.

GET MINTY FRESH

Brush your teeth and tongue with the best tasting toothpaste you can find. Use mouthwash and breath mints. You'll trick your taste buds.

ALWAYS EAT BREAKFAST

It fuels you for the day.
You'll be less hungry at lunch.

EMERGENCIES

AFTER A PIG OUT...

Don't beat yourself up. It happens to everyone, and it's easy to get back on track without much harm done.

EAT SOMETHING

Your first thought is to skip a meal or two. This will only make you feel worse, physically and emotionally

GET MOVING

Kick up your workout to take off those added calories.

   It also will make you feel better about yourself.

TAKE DEEP BREATHS

Try to clear your mind from the stresses of the day by taking deep breaths. Your stomach and diaphragm can get clenched from stress or tight clothing.

RELAX WITH MUSIC

It can get you in a good mood. It can make you cry. It will help you feel better about yourself.

PREVENTING A PIG OUT

- Know the warning signs. A fight with a friend or a bad grade may make you want to head for the ice cream. Try going for a relaxing walk instead.
- Have a back-up plan. Make a list of things that will take your mind off food.
- Make sure you reward yourself each time you win.

QUESTIONS AND ANSWERS

IS IT NECESSARY TO COUNT CALORIES?

I think it's next to impossible. If you plan on half a plate of vegetables and the main portion of the meal is no more than fist size, you should lose weight without having to consult a calorie chart.

IS IT IMPORTANT TO KEEP A FOOD JOURNAL?

Yes. Because you're much less likely to eat something if you know you have to write it down first.

WILL I LOSE WEIGHT IF I BECOME A VEGETARIAN?

Going vegetarian is not the answer to weight loss. Also, cutting meat from your diet eliminates a lot of iron and zinc, both of which are critical to teens.

SHOULD I ELIMINATE SALT?

A teaspoon of salt has no calories and no fat. Certain salty foods may add some weight, but it's temporary water weight.

Chapter 13

CELEBRITY SECRETS

Taking a close look at how some of your favorite celebrities put themselves together can help you create your own look.

BEAUTY TRICKS

Drew Barrymore's favorite beauty tool is a curling lash. Her lashes grow down, so she really "opens her eyes" with her curler. Drew likes to briefly heat the curler with her blow dryer so that the curl stays in.

Alyssa Milano's trademark is her perfectly shaped eyebrows. To achieve them she matches up her eye's iris and tapers them down to the corner of her outer eye.

Sarah Michelle Gellar emphasizes her eyes and lips with just the right amount of blush. She gets the right contour by following the lines of her cheekbones with her blush brush.

Gwyneth Paltrow plays up her eyes with sparkly gray eye shadow and a soft kohl gray pencil. She rims it around both her upper and lower lashes.

Jennifer Lopez uses shimmering creams and powders all over her body and face. Her lips are always highly glossed.

Courteney Cox Arquette keeps her skin looking flawless and oil free with rice paper powdered tissues. They can be found at drugstores or beauty supply shops.

Angie Harmon opens up her deep-set eyes with a well-groomed brow. It creates a lift and brings the eye forward. She chooses a light shadow and defined lash line.

Christina Aguilera widens her eyes by only applying shadow on the outer corners and lightening her eyelids with gloss.

CELEBRITY BODIES

Lisa Marie, actress and former model, only eats foods that give her energy and help her feel well. When she began eating this way, she stopped having to diet. She claims that when she eats healthfully—eating clean proteins and vegetables—she feels balanced and calm. She eats a lot of organic vegetables, fruits, homemade food, salmon, and salads. Her favorite teas are mint, green, and ginger. She satisfies her occasional sweet tooth with Twizzlers.

Sandra Bullock's secret to staying slim is to eat slowly. She usually finishes her meal ten minutes after her friends.

Gwyneth Paltrow stays slim with yoga.

Mariah Carey claims her dancing is strenuous exercise, and she gets a great workout on stage.

Beyoncé Knowles of Destiny's Child dances for thirty to forty-five minutes each day and does an amazing five hundred sit-ups. She boosts her energy with lots of water.

Renee Zellweger stretches and lunges to trim her abs and butt.

Rebecca Romijn-Stamos rates her favorite exercise as swimming, especially the freestyle stroke.

Sarah Jessica Parker bikes in Central Park and maintains her weight by having five to seven mini meals each day. Since she lives in New York, she walks everywhere. To get the most out her walking, Sarah Jessica squeezes her buttocks in each and every step. She believes a gym is not necessary when you're able to get outdoors.

Christina Applegate spins and keeps her energy up with orange juice.

Jennifer Love Hewitt loves kickboxing because it uses all her muscles and gives her energy.

Julia Roberts's one big meal of the day is always breakfast. She exercises by losing herself in dancing and jogging. Julia's favorite food? A big baked potato with fat-free cottage cheese, fresh herbs, and Butter Buds.

Angel star **Charisma Carpenter** loves healthy foods, especially cottage cheese. She tones her body by playing lots of tennis.

Jenna Elfman credits her body with taking ballet lessons three times a week, drinking ten glasses of water a day, avoiding sugar, and getting nine hours of sleep a night.

Tyra Banks loves playing basketball, especially doing jumps to tone her thighs and buttocks. She also jumps rope.

Jessica Alba comes from a family that is heavily overweight. She actually started cooking for herself at twelve so she would not have the same problems. Her day of eating is usually an egg white omelet and fruit or cottage cheese with a peach. For lunch she chooses a salad. Dinner is typically vegetables and chicken or fish. During the day she picks dried fruit or a frozen yogurt as a snack.

Here's good news. Even celebrities get sick of constant dieting and watching their weight. Look at **Jennifer Lopez**. Her weight tends to yo-yo, and yet she wears her clothes proudly no matter if it's up or down. The same goes for **Kate Winslet**, **Alicia Silverstone**, and a large cast of other celebrities who, in reality, are real people just like you!

CELEBRITY HAIR SECRETS

When **Julia Roberts** decides to go curly, she scrunches her hair with a curl-enhancing gel just after shampooing, and with a curling iron in a vertical direction.

Lucy Liu's great waves are the result of a blunt cut with slight layering at the ends for movement. Her hair is blown dry using a round brush, and pinned with larger pin curls. When the pins come out, her hair is gently finger-styled.

Drew Barrymore's secret hair trick for less-than-perfect hair days is to part her hair in the middle, pull one side back, and then secure it with a big sparkling barrette. You can find great ones at flea markets or use a big pin out of your grandmother's closet. Attach it to your hair with a couple of bobby pins.

Ananda Lewis' beautiful long hair is a combination of using Herbal Essences conditioning balm and this great secret. When she's having a bad hair day, she applies olive oil over the top of her hair to calm it down and give it shine.

Britney Spears's split ends get treated with almond oil. She rubs it between her palms, and applies it to the ends.

James King puts her own highlights in her hair. Here's how: she cuts the top of an old straw hat, pull her hair through the hole, then pours cooled Chamomile tea on her hair and sits out in the sun!

Mandy Moore adds shine to her hair with a whole egg and ½ cup honey. She put the mixture on dry hair, combs it through, and leaves it on for about an hour. Then she completely washes it out. It keeps her hair shiny and soft.

Molly Sims rates avocado as her favorite conditioner. She mashes a ripe avocado in a bowl, then applies it to unwashed hair. Molly leaves it on for twenty minutes before shampooing thoroughly.

Melissa Joan Hart loves the smell of lavender. Every day she applies lavender oil (available at health food stores and natural supermarkets) on her hair, concentrating on her ends to tame and scent.

Jennifer Aniston uses Mane 'n Tail shampoo that is also used to silken show horse's manes.

STYLE TRICKS

Supermodel **Kate Moss** is the perfect example of the look called "high-low." It's wearing a very expensive item with an inexpensive item. Another way of creating this look is to wear a cool vintage piece with very simple clothing. Kate loves to take a very expensive purse and wear it with jeans and sneakers. She's become a fashion guru with her unique style.

A style that is completely different, but definitely fun belongs to **Lil' Kim**. She dresses like no one else, like dressing as a snow bunny straight off the slopes, even with ski goggles. Hers is a style that only works when she's on stage. She may not be the best fashion role model for everyday wear, but her style is confident and inspiring. Copy from her the right to dress as you want and be yourself.

No Doubt's lead singer **Gwen Stefani**'s style is completely her own creation. She started developing her look by scouting thrift shops. Her style changes are the result of her mood changes. Whether it's baggy trousers with suspenders or embellished bras and zippers, her look is all her own.

CELEBRITY PROBLEMS & SOLUTIONS

Think you're the only one with bad skin or kinky hair? Everyone has them, even the most super of models.

Tara Reid minimizes large pores and gets rid of blackheads by using vitamin A powder mixed with her cleanser. It helps prevent pores from getting clogged.

Pro-surfing champ and model **Malia Jones** fixes the damage that the sun and the ocean inflicts on her hair by using hot oil treatments every week. To moisturize her body, Malia uses baby oil, perfect after a long day at the beach.

Model **Gisele Bundchen** never uses soap, only makeup remover and water to keep her skin from losing moisture.

Reese Witherspoon's hair tends to "puff" up. She manages her hair with castor oil to calm it down.

Tori Spelling loves to mix a tablespoon of lemon juice with a tablespoon of peroxide and apply it to damp hair. Then she sits out in the sun for twenty minutes to lighten it.

Mandy Moore had a lot of bad hair days growing up. She was the victim of too many permanents. Here's the conditioning trick that fixed her very damaged hair.

Pour jojoba oil all over dry hair, concentrating on the ends. Leave it on about ten minutes, then rinse it through with very warm water. Shampoo and condition lightly.

Jennifer Love Hewitt has always struggled with sweets, especially her mom's cupcakes. Now when her sweet tooth strikes, she grabs a piece of fruit.

Even **Jennifer Lopez**, just like most of us, gains weight first below the waist. Her solutions are to switch to protein shakes for a meal a day substitute, and she knows how to dress.

EXTRA CREDIT

- Skirts cut on the bias in a light fabric (like a knit) give a slim look.
- Long narrow skirts with a drop waist disguise a bulge.
- A tailored jacket with just enough padding to make your shoulders look wider than your hips can help.
- Wear pants that skim the body and fall just a bit long, and of course, darker is always more slimming.

Jamie-Lynn Sigler of *The Sopranos* works her hips and thighs out with lunges. She does them when she brushes her teeth, when she's memorizing her lines, and even at crossing lights. Try to ten on each leg, three times a day.

Model/actress **Rebecca Romijn-Stamos** hates doing ab work so much that she does two hundred crunches at a time, three times a week.

EXTRA CREDIT

Lie on your back with your hands behind your head. Lift your shoulders and extend your left leg as you bring your right knee in to your chest, touching it with your left elbow. Hold to the count of three. Switch sides and do the same. Do no more than 5 to 10 reps each, especially if you're just starting out.

STEAL HER LOOK

Jennifer Lopez has a style that has nothing to do with money.

- She picks only the colors that make her complexion look great—black, white, and beige.
- She always picks her most flattering neckline....the v-neck. It creates the illusion of a slimmer waist while making the neck look longer.
- Even though she wears a lot of jewelry, it's always small enough to not look overdone. It always looks like it must be real, even though sometimes it's not.
- She always wears something unexpected, something that shows that she is a true princess. It might be a gold toe ring, or the perfect barrette.

J. LO'S FAVORITE ACCESSORIES

Gold sunglasses

Bronzing stick

Shiny gloss

Lash curler

Halle Berry doesn't maintain her body with her No. 1 downfall, the love of potato chips. But she's not one to deny herself, so sensible Halle eats her chips baked. And she's trained her taste buds to enjoy low-fat pretzels.

Julia Roberts deals with her addiction to ice cream by opting for frozen yogurt or fruit ice pops. As a result, she cuts her calorie count by more than half.

Kelly Preston cut down on the breads and starches in her diet and changed to oatmeal and brown rice. Instead of saying no to snacks, she chooses fat-free Jell-O.

Alicia Silverstone has had a very public weight fluctuation. Now she stays in shape by cutting down on dairy products and switching to a low-fat, vegetarian diet. She's lost the baby fat and her skin cleared up.

Britney Spears treats her blemishes by steaming them with lemon herbal tea and boiling water. She boils a big pot and puts her face over it until it cools. It also clears clogged pores.

Janet Jackson's problem was loving to eat, and especially loving to eat out. She even admits to having battled bulimia and anorexia. She dramatically changed her appearance by switching to a vegetarian-based diet, and she started running, doing sit-ups, and boxing.

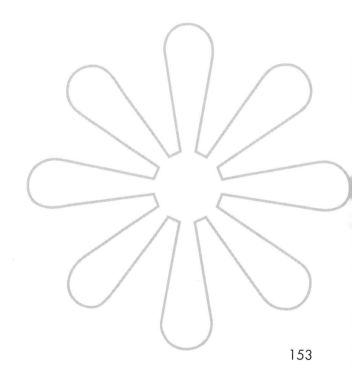

Chapter 14

TEEN
HAIR

BASIC HAIR

Your hair is a fun way to experiment with your looks. It's an easy way to change how you look in a matter of minutes. Look around. Do you see a haircut on a person with hair texture that's similar to yours? Check it out. Then go home to try the style on yourself.

Teen hair can take a lot of experimentation because hair is extremely healthy right now. Your best bet is to play around with temporary solutions. There are lots of temporary hair products that will allow you to discover the look that's best for you.

You don't need to spend a lot on hair products to have great hair. You'll find very good shampoos, conditioners, brushes, rollers, and just about any other styling product you can think of at drugstores and discount stores.

IT'S NOT **COMPLICATED**

The better the haircut, the healthier the hair. A good haircut will allow you to go through the day, the weather, and whatever else happens, with hair that still looks great.

HOW IMPORTANT?

When our hair looks good, everything else works. We feel confident and secure.

When it frizzes and flops around, it can totally ruin our mood.

PRACTICE, **HAVE FUN**, PRACTICE

It's all the same. Remember when you would try different hairstyles and occasionally even haircuts on your dolls? Wasn't it fun? Well, I wouldn't try any hair-cutting, but getting together with friends or sitting in front of the mirror will make you see how you can change your looks with a few strategically placed strands.

DON'T FIGHT NATURE

If you've been blessed with incredible curls, don't get too hung up on keeping it stick straight. Try a "curly" day. See how you like it. Listen to the comments. Watch the reactions. Your hair may look the best the way it was intended to go. It's fun to try new things, and you can always change back. That girl you admire because her hair is so fine and silky? Perhaps she's been wishing for your thick hair.

HAIR TOOLS

The right tools create the right look. The hair tools you use can make the difference in the styling, health, and maintenance of your everyday look. Here's what you need.

BRUSH

A good quality brush is the basis of your hair wardrobe.

A natural bristle like boar's hair is worth the purchase. Animal bristles work like your hair—they are porous and they sort the natural oils from your scalp and spread them throughout your hair. In this way your hair oils will be distributed throughout and provide shine.

Choose a synthetic brush if your hair is very thick and tends to tangle. Synthetic bristles, which are usually made of nylon, are stronger and are more effective at getting rid of knots and taming unruly hair.

If you have a lot of highlights, consider a metal brush to keep the shine.

For smoothing, an oversized paddle brush is perfect. It helps keep hair flat and is also good for drying long hair because you can grab a lot of strands at a time.

HAIR **DRYER**

Choose one that's comfortable to hold, with enough heat to seal the cuticle. A dryer with 1875 watts is a good value. Different speeds are a good option.

Look for the "cool shot" feature. It's a button that lets you blast your locks with cold air to seal the cuticle and get rid of frizz. It also helps boost shine.

CHOOSING THE RIGHT SHAMPOO

COARSE/KINKY HAIR

This is the driest hair type, so look for moisturizing shampoos. Shea butter, coconut oils, and macadamia nut are some ingredients to look for.

FINE/LIMP HAIR

Shampoos that state they are volumizing work, and so do very clear shampoos, which usually will contain volume-building ingredients, like panthenol and protein.

WAVY/CURLY HAIR

This hair type tends to be dry, so choose a cream formulated shampoo with ingredients like propylene glycol and lauryl sulfate.

HAIR PRODUCTS

It's always important to check the labels of your hair products. Certain ingredients will provide certain results.

If you want great gloss, check the labels for products containing jojoba or aloe. These ingredients are effective in providing shine without grease.

To get your hair straight, look for citrus ingredients. These products should contain ingredients like grapefruit, orange, and lime. They help straighten hair and help to prevent waving caused by moisture.

To increase volume in your hair, look for ingredients like polymers. These are synthetic molecules that expand the natural space between hairs to give strands extra lift.

To fight frizz, products should contain proteins, which help stabilize the natural proteins in your own hair.

To soften hair, your product should contain silicone. This helps to strengthen and moisturize hair, as well as protect it from styling products that use heat.

HAIR COLOR

Maybe you were born with beautiful light blonde hair, but all of a sudden puberty hit and your color is starting to turn a dull brown. Or you never liked your color, and you want a change.

There are lots of ways to make fun changes.

SEMIPERMANENT

It's a good way to experiment. If you don't like it, it won't damage your hair, and you won't be stuck with it.

HIGHLIGHT

If you can afford it, try a professional. If you can't then ask a friend or your mom to do it for you. Adding a few streaks to your hair is a fun way to get started. Plus, there are several "at home" coloring kits that are inexpensive and have really complete, easy-to-follow instructions.

WASH OUT COLOR

These last about four weeks, and can help you decide if you're really meant to be a redhead.

WIG OUT!

It's a painless way to see if you like that hair color. It's also a great preview to a new hairstyle.

TALK TO YOUR PARENTS FIRST

There's not a hair color in the world

that's worth getting in trouble over.

HAIR SEASONS

SUMMER

Heat-proof your hair and stop your color from fading.

Your products should have UV filters.

Wear a hat.

Use a color-protecting shampoo.

After swimming in the pool, rinse your hair in apple cider vinegar to remove the chlorine.

STEAMY SCALP

Use a mint shampoo or conditioner. It will actually lower your scalp's temperature.

WINTER

If your hair is covered with snow, don't comb it out until it dries.

Shake off the excess water and snow.

If your hair has frozen (it can happen!), put your hair dryer on low and thaw it out.

PROTECT YOUR HAIR

with a good silicone finishing treatment.

PRO SECRETS

FIGHT FRIZZ

Just spritz damp hair with a light conditioning spray. Then let your hair air dry, or blow it dry on low or with a diffuser.

COWLICK CONTROL

After you've styled your hair, wet the cowlick and position it in place.

Keep it there with a wax or pomade.

HEALTHY HAIR

Use a nourishing mask at least once a week. You'll find them in drugstores with names like "deep" treatment.

BED HEAD

Love that look that you've seen on the runways? Vary the amount of styling cream you use all over your head. It will create a multi-textured effect.

CONTROL YOUR CURLS

Use a heated comb. Set it on low to medium and run it over any area that you need to smooth.

HAVE A TRIM

Even if you are trying to grow your hair out, you need to have your hair trimmed every four to six weeks. It will get rid of dead split ends and even helps your hair grow faster.

TREAT YOUR HAIR LIKE A SALAD

A hot oil treatment makes your hair shiny and manageable. Just use olive oil.

Warm it up and coat your dry, unwashed hair with it. Sit out in the sun for twenty minutes.

Wash it out thoroughly and condition.

CHOOSING THE RIGHT STYLE

Hair stylists cut hair…that's what they're trained to do. They're not psychic. If you want a certain look, you need to bring a picture.

You also need to tell your stylist that you want no more than half an inch, one inch, etc. They should hold up the length they're planning to cut so that you'll be comfortable.

SHORT HAIR REASONS

- Getting ready quicker
- Flatters a pretty face
- Highlights cheekbones
- Gives more attention to small features

LONG HAIR PLUSSES

- More versatile
- Less apt to frizz
- Slims a face

STRAIGHT HAIR BENEFITS

- Chic
- Polished
- Looks natural

CURLY HAIR CAUSES

- Romantic
- Gives more volume
- Wash and go

BRAID BONUSES

- Low-maintenance
- Style statement
- Cutting edge

GREAT HAIR ON A BUDGET

USE COLD WATER

Make your final rinse a cold one. It will really make your hair shine.

DETOX YOUR PRODUCTS

Add a couple of aspirin to your shampoo to take out all the excess product and get your hair squeaky clean.

GET RID OF OIL

Dip your fingers in baking soda and massage your scalp to instantly dry up oil. It's a great way to revive your style.

LEND A HAND

If you want to tame flyaways and give your hair a little shine, run some hand lotion over it.

Just rub the lotion in the palms of your hands, and then run your palms over your hair. Don't use too much lotion or it will look greasy.

COLORING TIPS

The ends of your hair are more porous and soak up more color than the roots. Rub conditioner over the ends while your hair is processing. The last five minutes, apply color to the ends, over the conditioner. The color will penetrate just enough to create an even color.

SHAMPOO YOUR HAIR the day before you color your hair so that your hair color will go on without streaks.

For root touch up (and nothing else), part your hair into four equal sections.

Keep the sections in place with bobby pins or clips.

Apply the color to the parts themselves.

Take each section and work on the roots of the section, and then clip up again.

This keeps the coloring on the root, and keeps you from wasting product.

Use a shampoo with a low pH level so that it won't strip out your color.

EXTRA CREDIT
If your shampoo doesn't lather very much, it's low pH.

Peroxide-based acne treatments like Sea Breeze can give very subtle highlights. Use a toothbrush and simply apply product to thin sections of hair. Let it sit ten minutes and shampoo thoroughly.

Just the way the sun can fade hair, so can blow dryers, curling irons, and flat irons. Try to find products with thermal protectors. These products have barriers to protect hair.

ALWAYS RINSE
with cool water after every wash to extend the life of your color.

SALON SECRETS

Finding a stylist can be very difficult, especially for a teen. Very often teens are afraid to speak out when their hair doesn't look like they expected. Here's some advice.

Look for friends and even strangers who have great hair. First tell them they look great, and then ask who their stylist is. Don't be shy; they'll appreciate the compliment.

If you want to try a new salon, schedule a consultation first. This will give you a chance to find out that you and your stylist are on the same wavelength. A great stylist will listen to you and make suggestions right away.

Bring pictures of the look that you like. No

matter how you describe what you want, a picture tells a thousand words.

IF YOUR FACE IS ROUND,

your stylist should stay away from most chin length styles. A mid-neck bob slightly layered or a shoulder-length style is good for your face shape.

SQUARE FACES SHOULD

go with a longer cut with face fringing.

HAIR FUN

Recycle your panty hose and make your own scrunchies.

Cut your hose in three- to four-inch lengths. You'll love the way you can match your hair color, and your hair will not be snagged or pulled as with an elastic band.

BE INVENTIVE with your jewelry

Rings can be hair ties.

Pins can become barrettes.

HAIR CARE

QUICK TRICK

Women of color tend to have oily scalps and dry, coarse hair. Here's a way to distribute the oils as well as give hair a quick look of renewal.

Take a brush and the force the bristles through a section of clean panty hose.

Brush hair from the roots to the ends.

CONDITIONING OIL TREATMENTS

Shea butter

Almond oil

Avocado oil

Olive oil

Take as much as you need, usually about a half-cup, and pour it over your head before shampooing. Let it set for about ten to twenty minutes. Shampoo and condition as usual.

HAIR CRISES

YOUR BANGS ARE GETTING TO THAT SHEEPDOG STAGE

Dampen your hair, and comb forward the bangs that go from the middle of one eyebrow to the center of the other. Pull tight and cut right at the bridge of your nose. Your bangs will pop back up to your brows in a natural line.

YOUR ROOTS ARE SHOWING

Make a zig zag part.

Cover with chalk or washable magic marker.

YOUR LAYERS ARE TOTALLY OVERGROWN

Use the top layers you're trying to grow out to create extra volume. After drying, spritz roots at the crown with spray gel. Tease a bit to create fullness.

YOUR ENDS ARE RAGGED

Blow dry while using a round brush to flip ends up. For extra hold, blow with cool air and spritz with hairspray.

YOUR LAYERS HAVE A MIND OF THEIR OWN

Control layers by applying a super hold gel to damp hair then combing through.

Secure layers with a clip and allow hair to air dry.

YOUR COMB KEEPS GETTING STUCK IN YOUR TANGLES

Dampen hair and then straighten out, starting from the ends.

YOUR HAIR HAS THAT "STEAMROLLED" LOOK

Blow out hair straight and then set it for a few minutes in hot rollers to give it more volume.

YOUR HAIR IS A DISASTER

Braid it. It's a cute look, and no one has to know what's underneath.

Chapter 15

MODEL LOOKS

WHAT DOES A MODEL REALLY LOOK LIKE?

Everyone has flaws, including the world's most famous models. I should know. I've been a model, and I've been with them up close and personal. The difference between them and everyone else is that they know how to minimize and hide their flaws. You can learn those skills too.

IT'S HARD WORK

There are hours of preparation, a strict lifestyle, and a lot of scrutiny. Take for instance, a foot model. Seems like the perfect job, right? It must be fun trying on different shoes all day. What you don't hear about are the swollen feet at night. A foot model never walks around barefoot (even in the summer) because she needs to protect her feet at all times. But the good news is that you don't have to go through every minute of a model's life. And it's good to know that you can take some of the secrets and use them when you need them.

SOME THINGS ARE NOT WHAT THEY SEEM

If you see a model with a tattoo, don't assume it's a permanent one. Temporary tattoos are widely used, because, quite simply, most agencies don't allow tattoos. The models that have them usually have to cover them up.

You can find temporary tattoos at lots of stores, especially costume and novelty shops.

They're fun and painless, and totally removable.

There are also salons that will do a henna tattoo. It lasts longer (two to four weeks) than the tattoos that just wash off after a day or two.

MODEL'S TRICKS

CINDY CRAWFORD

Cindy keeps her skin fresh and moist by making a spritzer using equal amounts of milk and bottled water. She puts it into a spray bottle and shakes it up. After spraying, she just wipes the excess off with a tissue.

TYRA BANKS

Tyra is honest and helpful to admitting to having a bad habit of nail biting. She has a great trick of dipping her fingers in vinegar or Tabasco sauce. It definitely keeps her fingers out her mouth.

JAMES KING

Her favorite lip moisturizer is honey, which she applies over her lipstick for extra shine. Then she gently blots it so that it looks like it's part of her lipstick.

HOW DO THEY KEEP THOSE DRESSES ON?

Just how do the models keep their very bare dresses on the runway? How do Jennifer Lopez and Courtney Love look so confident on the red carpet?

Here's how they get their very little whatever's to stay put. Tuf Skin, a spray-on adhesive for bandages, does the trick. Beauty contestants also use it to keep their bathing suits in place. You should be able to find it easily in most drugstores, or the First Aid aisle of most discount stores.

MODEL'S TRICKS FOR TAKING GREAT PICTURES

Fool the flash of the camera by using matte makeup or powder. The only place for shine in a picture is on your lips.

Don't wear white. White is the worst color to wear in photos because it enhances the flash. A little color makes the picture (and you) look better.

Do something! Lean over, put your hand under your chin, and don't forget to pose your body in an angle. An angle will give the picture more depth and interest.

Try not to have your picture taken in the sun. The picture won't come out very well, and the sun is not flattering to anyone, no matter how beautiful.

CLOSE SHOTS

If a picture is a close up, and you want to look like a natural beauty, and don't want to live down those yearbook pictures in years to come, be sure to check the following.

- Keep eyebrows in place by spraying them with hairspray.
- Remove any visible hair on your face and body.
- Make sure your clothing is thoroughly ironed.
- All hair wisps should be sprayed or gelled down.
- Make sure whatever you wear has been test-driven.

Wake up your **COMPLEXION** with an ice cube. Rub it over your face and watch the circulation increase. That's a glow, girl.

MODEL MAKEUP SECRETS

BLEMISH DISGUISING

- Prepare the area with a drop of moisturizer mixed with a drop of or two of eye redness reliever. This will allow the concealer to properly stick to the skin.
- Next, take a very small brush and dip into concealer. Gently brush over the blemish.
- Apply foundation. Then reapply concealer.
- Gently pat over with loose powder to keep the blemish covered.

PERFECT (LOOKING) SKIN

To create the look of flawless skin, wrap a pressed powder puff around your pointer finger. Dip it into loose powder and carefully roll it onto your skin.

HIGH CHEEKBONES

Models give the illusion of high cheekbones by applying foundation one shade deeper than their regular foundation shade. They apply it just under the cheekbone.

BIGGER EYES

Use a pale, shimmery eye shadow in a peach or pink shade on the lid and in the inner corner of the eye, right near the bridge of the nose. It creates a brightening effect. It's perfect by itself, or over another eye shadow color.

Here's the **MODEL'S WAY** to curl your lashes. Clamp your curler at the base of your lashes and then "walk" it out to the tip. Be sure to clamp down along the way.

Luscious Lips

- Open a vitamin E capsule with a pin and squeeze the contents on your fingertip. Use it as a gloss and to treat chapped lips. Wipe off the flakes with a toothbrush.

- Coat lips with foundation and let it dry.

- Apply lip-gloss and blot.

Hold your mascara wand vertically while applying mascara for more volume. This also replaces liner because this method creates a natural line.

Wake up your eyes by applying eyeliner thinly at the inner eye and thicker at the outer eye.

Always soften your liner after applying it with a cotton swab. Pat over the line to achieve the smoky effect.

Seal your eyeliner with powdered shadow in a closely matching shade.

LIP TRICKS

Always wipe off lip balm before applying lipstick. Lips must be clean or the lipstick will go on unevenly.

Never apply a hard lip pencil to lips. Soften the tip by warming it up for a few seconds between your fingers.

Make lips look smaller by applying concealer on lip rim.

Draw an outline that's just inside the natural lip line.

Keep lipstick off teeth by inserting a tissue into your mouth with your finger and then drawing out excess lipstick.

NATURAL LOOKING LIPS

When models need to look like they have no makeup on, here's what they do. Apply lip balm and then apply neutral pencil over it.

PETROLEUM JELLY GIVES LIPS A NATURAL GLOSS.

BLEND LIPSTICK into cheeks for a natural glow. Use your finger so that the heat of your body temperature will help blend in the color. Never go beyond the outer corner of the eyes.

GET THE PERFECT BLUSH COLOR

Match your blush to the skin inside your lower lip.

SHADOW TRICK

Have your eye shadow perform double duty. Apply it wet to get a smoky look.

Don't use water because it will crack once it's dry. Apply a drop of eye redness reliever to your brush, and then dip into the shadow. This is done at photo shoots because the eye redness reliever turns the powder into a paste. It looks perfect and, even better, it lasts.

MODEL HAIR TRICKS

QUICK TRICKS FOR FLAT HAIR

Simply switch your part to the opposite side. It gives hair an instant lift.

Comb styling gel through slightly damp hair. Twist sections around your finger and hold them with clips. Blow dry on the lowest setting. Remove the clips, and lift your hair at the roots.

Turn your head upside down and blow dry hair while fluffing. Flip over and smooth the cuticle.

SHINY HAIR

Spray anti-frizz/shine serum on a large fluffy makeup brush. Use the largest brush you can find, and make sure it's only used for hair. Brush it all over hair.

Rub a bit of hair conditioner in your hands and gently pat all over your head.

**Avoid leaving a
DENT IN YOUR HAIR
by slipping a tissue under your hair clips
while applying makeup.**

STRAIGHT HAIR

Here's how to get hair perfectly straight without a flat iron.

Clip hair against one side of your head and blow dry.

Repeat on the other side of your head.

⭐ **EXTRA CREDIT**

Keep a comb between your flat iron and your scalp so you don't burn yourself.

When **STRAIGHTENING** hair with a blow dryer, start at the ends and work your way up. Always **POINT THE DRYER** down on top of the hair to seal in the cuticle and make the hair flatter.

MODEL BODY TRICKS

MODEL LEGS

Keep weight on one leg, and bring your other leg forward so one foot is crossed in front of the other, then bend your knee slightly to create a slim line.

Wear sheer dark hose. Light colors make legs look heavier.

Models prevent razor rash by loosening hairs before shaving. Scrubbing with a **LOOFAH** or coarse washcloth also takes away the top layer of skin to allow a smooth surface for shaving.

DARK SKIN PATCHES

Apply a lemon half to knees and heels where skin is thicker and darker. The citric acid bleaches and softens. Let it set for ten to fifteen minutes. Rinse off with a wet washcloth.

SOFT SKIN

Models get super soft legs for those extra close close-ups by applying a face mask. Use it once a week all over your legs. Let it set for ten minutes and then rinse off in the shower.

PHOTO FINISH SHAVE

To shave like the models do, shave in the morning when legs are less puffy. Let legs absorb water for a couple of minutes to open up the follicles. Use hair conditioner for a smoother shave. Rinse legs in cold water to close the pores.

FIRM LEGS

Here's what models do before a swimsuit shoot to make their legs look sleek and slim.

Apply dried seaweed sheets to wet legs. It's available at health food stores and natural supermarkets. Apply a blow dryer until the seaweed dries. Then peel off seaweed.

CELLULITE REMOVER

Models apply warm coffee grounds (make sure it's have caffeinated). They massage it in with a vegetable brush in a circular motion, let it set for five minutes, then rinse off.

STANDING IN HIGH HEELS

Tape your second toe (the one next to your big toe) on top of your third toe to help high heels feel more comfortable. This trick takes some pressure off the feet.

Secrets of Leg Models

- Don't cross your legs. It hurts circulation and causes spider veins.

- Massage your legs with lotion every night in a circular motion.

- Use creams containing cocoa butter.

- Sleep in cotton leggings after applying a thick layer of lotion. In the morning your legs will be super smooth.

PHOTO SHOOT TRICK

Apply hair shine serum to your legs.

Mix hair serum with a little bronzing powder, concentrating on shins and the tops of the thighs. This highlights the bones and creates definition.

MODEL ARMS

Models use face-firming masks to tighten their arms. Simply apply the mask to the backs of your arms and let it dry. Then rinse off.

Models get rid of bumps on the back of their arms by using AHA creams.

To heal BRUISES quickly, break open a vitamin K capsule and tap the contents into the bruise.

INGROWN HAIRS

See those little bumps on your knees and bikini line? They're actually ingrown hairs.

Get rid of them by scrubbing the area with a mesh shower puff. Use a circular motion.

RUNWAY HAIR

Models, who are going for that "at the beach" look, take a clear, carbonated soda like Sprite and pour it into a spray bottle. Then they lightly spray it on the end of curly or wavy hair.

To make hair immediately shiny and get residue out, make a paste of baking soda and water. Apply it to the hair for twenty minutes. Rinse out thoroughly. This is especially good for getting rid of chlorine after photo shoots that involve posing in chlorinated swimming pools.

Make your style stay styling a little longer by keeping fingers, brushes, and styling products out of your hair for less buildup.

Refresh your style with a blow dryer set on cool.

Bring hair BACK TO LIFE by rolling in opposite directions.

RUNWAY LEGS

To make models legs look instantly tan, we rub a dry oil mixed with bronzing powder all over the legs.

If there's more time, a self-tanner is used, mixed with a small amount of moisturizer to ensure an even appearance.

MODEL EATING

Trust me, model eating is not just diet soda and bubble gum. There are lots of tricks that models use.

Gisele Bundchen gets that "oh-my-good-ness-how-did-she-get-that-body" look by eating the way most models from Brazil do. For breakfast, she has fruit, grain bread, and coffee. The largest meal of the day is lunch: salad, fish or meat, quinoa, and dessert. And for dinner, she helps herself to stew, salad, bread, and cheese.

Heidi Klum drinks soy shakes and runs wind sprints before those Victoria Secret shows.

MUSTS FOR MODELS BEFORE A PHOTO SHOOT

Never skip breakfast.
Don't go more than four hours without eating.
Fill half of plates with vegetables.

THE DAY BEFORE

Drink as much water as possible to detox.
Add an extra workout.

MODEL EMERGENCIES

OVER PLUCKING

Sometimes makeup artists go overboard and pluck, pluck, pluck away. It can get so bad that the models can't remember what their natural brow originally looked like. When this happens to you try the following:

- Leave your brows alone for three weeks to see if the hairs will grow back.
- Comb brows up and out. Snip off any extra long hairs.
- Don't go outside the brow line, but use a soft pencil to fill in very sparse spots.
- Shadow over the brow in a closely matched shade so the brow won't look so harsh.

NO BRA, NO PROBLEM

Models carry tape for such occasions. One or two strips of electrical tape goes from one armpit to the other. Just follow where the bottom of your bra would go. Destick the tape on some fabric or plain white paper so that it doesn't hurt when it's pulled off.

NOSE BUMPS

Lots of models have slight bumps that can easily be disguised. After applying foundation, dip a brush into eye shadow that's slightly darker than your skin tone. On each side your nose; draw a light line along the sides, stopping at the bridge. Tap a little on top of the nose.

INSTANT GROOMED BROWS

Tack brows up with a little soap and water. Don't use too much or you'll look constantly surprised.

BREAKOUT PREVENTION

Models who tend to break out, and know they have to model the next day, eat one or two antacid tablets before going to bed.

These balance the acid in the skin and help to stop breakouts.

BREAKOUT RASH

Apply sliced cucumbers to the rash. They have anti-inflammatory properties to tone down redness. Apply tea tree oil as a toner.

SHAVING EMERGENCY

Put pressure on the cut for five minutes with a tissue soaked in a nasal decongestant spray like Afrin, which stops blood flow by constricting blood vessels.

THIN LIPS

A small amount of gloss or pearlized eye shadow in the center of the bottom lip will make the lips appear pouty and fuller.

EXTRA CREDIT
Dab light eye shadow or highlighting cream right above the bow of the lip and blend slightly.

TIRED EYES

When model's eyes become bloodshot, a cotton ball saturated with eye drops that is kept in the fridge is gently placed on the eyelid.

It cools the eyes and makes the redness disappear in less than a minute.

MAKEUP SMUDGES

Use this model's technique to refresh your eye makeup without having to reapply the whole thing. Use a cotton swab and non-oily makeup remover to take off any makeup that has smudged under your eyes. Then lightly pat on an alcohol-free toner and concealer.

Chapter 16

INTERNATIONAL BEAUTY

Have you ever been curious about what they do in other parts of the world to become and stay beautiful?

Will these tips work for you? Sure! They're fun, and they've passed through generations. Plus, we all have genetic origins from other parts of the world. So if your heritage is from a certain culture, then it just follows that the advice could be applicable.

ITALY

Teens are instructed by their moms and grand-mas to keep their eyelashes from breaking by applying castor oil at night.

CHINA

Take one-teaspoon rosemary oil, and mix it with a cup of green tea. Then pour it over your head as a final rinse for hair that really shines.

GREECE

Grecian teens head to the beach where they oil their bodies with baby oil, exfoliate their skin with sand, and rinse it all off in the ocean. Of course, they apply their sunscreen before laying out.

POLAND

Honey is used as a beauty product. Although their moms warm it and apply it all over their faces as a super moist facial treatment, Polish teens use honey as a lip-softening treatment.

INDIA

Yogurt and almonds are an every-night necessity. Grind ten almonds to a pulp with a mallet, and then add just enough whole yogurt to make it easy to spread. This beauty mask is applied to a clean face and left on for twenty-five minutes. Then it's wiped off with cheesecloth and rinsed.

EGYPT

Keep teeth white and beautiful with a combination of baking soda and coarse salt. Apply it with your fingers and let it set a minute.

AUSTRALIA

Girls here love to walk barefoot and wear toe-revealing sandals. To achieve flawless feet, they rub avocado skins all over their rough spots.

SPAIN

Spanish teens sometimes party just a bit too much. When they have the dark circles to show their good time, they take a potato and cut it very thinly. Then they apply it on the eyes for ten minutes, allowing the juice to seep into the darkness.

JAMAICA

These Caribbean beauties treat their skin with banana peels. They rub the peels over their face to soften and protect from the sun. They also use it on sunburned areas.

SCOTLAND

Fair girls from this country have very sensitive skin. They use almond oil after cleansing.

RUSSIA

On the coldest days, Russian teens express their style with jeans and the best coat they can buy. And when they cut themselves shaving, they rub garlic cloves on the affected area. Garlic contains antibacterial compounds.

JAPAN

Seaweed is the big secret in beauty here. It's sold at supermarkets and is prized for its cleansing and toning, and its ability to make the skin glow. Teens here use it on their bodies for cellulite, on their faces as masks, and eat it in their salads to help their hair grow.

DID YOU KNOW?
IN ANCIENT JAPAN TEENS BLACKENED THEIR TEETH AS A STATUS OF BEAUTY?

AFRICA

In some areas of Africa, teens pour milk over their heads and let their hair soak every other day for twenty minutes before shampooing.

KOREA

Generations of Korean teens treat dry areas with kukui-nut oil, which comes from a native tree.

TURKEY

Turkish teens eat a lot of kefir, a fermented milk product similar to yogurt. You can get the same benefits by choosing yogurt with live cultures. They help you break down food and get more nutrients from your food.

TAIWAN

These teens not only drink a lot of tea, they swab it on their body to cool sunburn. The tannic acid alleviates the sting.

FRANCE

French teens are more resistant to tooth decay because they eat cheese. It contains substances that strengthen tooth enamel and neutralize plaque.

SWEDEN

Swedish beauties eat wild blueberries with cereal and meats as their No. 1 beauty food.

International Fresh Breath

In **GREECE** they chew anise seeds to freshen their breath.

In **PORTUGAL** it's basil for close-ups.

ISRAELI teens chew sage.

GUATEMALANS chew cardamom.

In **INDIA** the breath mint of choice is fennel.

FRENCH teens eat their parsley.

INTERNATIONAL PORTIONS VS. AMERICAN PORTIONS

In the United States, food portions are huge when compared to the quantity of food served in other countries. When you go out to eat, try eating international style.

ITALY

Pasta serving: 10 ounces/800 calories
U.S.: 20 ounces/1600 calories
Cappuccino: 5 ounces/50 calories
U.S.: 12 ounces/145 calories

In Italy, you'll eat a six-course meal, but each is served on a separate plate. By eating one food at a time, Italians become satisfied with the food's flavor more quickly and eat less.

Americans mix foods and tastes on one plate so it takes longer (and more food) to feel satisfied.

FRANCE

Croissant: 2 ounces/210 calories
U.S.: 4 ounces/420 calories
Chocolate truffle .25 ounce/40 calories
U.S.: 1.5 ounces/220 calories

MEXICO

Taco serving: 2.5 ounces/180 calories
U.S.: 5 ounces/260 calories

JAPAN

Sushi serving: 2 ounces/80 calories
U.S.: 4 ounces/160 calories

Chapter 17

MAKING UP

FIRST MAKEUP

Wearing makeup for the first time may set off the urge to pile it on. You'll only end up looking like a little girl playing in her mother's room. Of course, you need to experiment. That's the fun of making up. Applying too much makeup, however, will not make you look older; it will only make you look like someone who doesn't know what she's doing. Make sure you practice, practice, and then practice some more. Your face is unique, different from any other face in the world. Once you learn the curves and planes in your face, you'll be able to put your makeup on expertly and quickly.

PREPARE AHEAD

Before you put any makeup on, make sure your face is washed and toned. Healthy skin is the first step to a beautiful face.

START LIGHT

The easiest way to experiment is with light, sheer colors. Starting this way, if you make a mistake, it's not so noticeable. Plus, today's looks favor natural colors.

Another reason to go sheer is that you don't have to be an expert in color. Sheer colors are suitable for all skin types.

TEENS CAN GET AWAY WITH MORE!

Young skin can get away with glitter, tropical colors, or even no makeup at all if you prefer. What will look amazing on you will look crazy on someone older.

DON'T CHANGE

Learn to enhance what you were born with.

The way you dress your face says a lot about who you are and what you want the world to see. Use makeup to enhance yourself, not to totally recreate yourself. The great thing about makeup is that you can change your look according to where you're going. The time of day also makes a difference in the kind of makeup you wear, and your own personality always should be evident.

GENERAL RULES

As a general guideline, keep daytime makeup natural looking. Too much makeup or the wrong makeup only will make you look worse when your intent is to look better. Play around, but don't get carried away.

MAKEUP RULES TO LIVE BY

CONSIDER THE WEATHER

A full face of makeup looks and feels ridiculous in the hot heat of summer. Pastels and glosses fade out in the cold dark days of winter.

YOUR SURROUNDINGS

Since you wouldn't wear the same clothes to school that you would to a party, you shouldn't wear the same makeup. Match your face to your wardrobe.

TIME OF DAY

Different lighting means you need different makeup. Daytime light is stronger, so you will need less makeup in the day. Nighttime has less light so you should use stronger colors.

YOUR SKIN

When you are having a bad skin day, you'll need more coverage to even things out. When your skin looks great, you may not even need makeup.

If you get a tan or change your hair color, you'll need to change your makeup accordingly.

YOUR COMFORT LEVEL

If you're wearing something on your face that doesn't make you feel and look awesome, forget about it. It may be for the next girl, but it's not for you. Keep practicing with the basics and then you can move on to the more complicated stuff.

For instance, if you have braces, you may not feel comfortable with a very dark lipstick because it will bring too much attention to your mouth. Plus it may end up on your wires. Stay with the lip-gloss.

If you really love BRIGHT COLORS, keep them to one area of your face. In this way, you'll be able to wear a bright color without looking like a clown.

CHOOSING THE RIGHT COLORS

You'll want to start collecting cosmetics slowly and thoughtfully so that you don't end up with cabinets full of stuff that looked great at the store but you never actually use.

YOUR COLOR IS IN YOUR HANDS

Actually, it's on the underside of your wrists. That's where skin undertones are most apparent. You have cool tones if your skin in this area is shaded with reds or blues. You are suited for warm tones if yellow and orange shades your skin.

THE SCARF TEST

Tie a pink scarf, then an orange scarf around your neck. If the orange scarf looks better, you probably look best in gold or yellow tones. If you look better in the pink scarf, pink under-tones will work better for you.

This applies to everyone regardless of eye color, hair color, or ethnicity.

Fair skin usually looks best in blue-based shades.

Medium skin can wear most shades.

Dark skin is most flattered by yellow-based shades and true red lipsticks.

CHECK YOUR VEINS

If the veins on your inner wrist are a greenish shade, then you're a warm.

Bluer veins mean you have cool tones.

TRY ON SOME JEWELRY

Slip on a gold necklace, then a silver one.

If the gold looks better then your skin tones are warm.

Does the silver look better? You're cool.

FOUNDATION MATCHING

Find a **FOUNDATION** with sunscreen.

TEENS rarely need pink-based foundations. Yellow-based colors look more natural.

Pick two or three shades that match your skin. Draw a streak on your **JAWLINE**, and see which matches best. If there's no tester, hold the bottles up to your jaw.

When you're caught between two shades, go for the slightly **DARKER** one.

Shop where you can make returns. Keep your **RECEIPTS** until you're sure your new make up is right for you. Most drugstores and cosmetic counters honor this policy.

Get samples if you can, or use the in-store **TESTERS** and wear the product home to see how it looks in your own bathroom mirror or outside.

LAYING A FOUNDATION

Getting the right foundation is critical to the entire look. It's like building a house.

Tinted Moisturizer

This is the lightest foundation, with very little coverage. Smooth it over your face as you would a moisturizer.

Liquid Foundation

Gives a sheer coverage and leaves time for blending.

Stick Foundation

A cream foundation with medium coverage. It also can be used as a concealer.

Cream to Powder

A non-oily foundation that dries to a matte finish. Apply it with a sponge.

Foundation Powder

A two-in-one foundation that can be used with a damp sponge for heavy coverage or with a brush for a lighter finish.

DON'T HESITATE TO COMBINE TWO OR EVEN THREE SHADES OF FOUNDATION TO GET THE COLOR YOU NEED. ALWAYS MIX IT IN THE PALM OF YOUR HAND, NEVER ON YOUR FACE.

ALL ABOUT APPLYING

- Start with perfectly clean skin and a little bit of moisturizer to help you spread the foundation.
- Dot first on blemishes or reddened areas.
- Begin in the middle of the face, smoothing with clean fingers or a sponge.
- Extend the foundation to under the chin.

- Apply extra foundation or concealer if needed.
- Only apply powder to extra oily areas, like the nose and chin.

THE WAY TO BLEND

The problem with foundation for women of color is that the skin tone is not always even. The best way to find the right foundation is to buy the shades that are slightly lighter and slightly darker than your skin tone, and blend.

CONCEALER

The right choice for women with deep olive or darker skin is a concealer with a yellow-orange base. Stay away from green because it doesn't blend well with darker skin. Also stay away from pink or peach because they are for lighter undertones.

The yellow tone blocks out dark circles under the eyes. Then add an orange-toned color for warmth. Buy two shades and blend them together. Put a dot of each color in the palm of your hand and run a blow dryer over it to help it more easily blend, and to make the concealer easier to apply.

DON'T PAINT YOUR CONCEALER ON. GENTLY TAP IT ON, CONCENTRATING ON THE INNER AND OUTER CORNERS OF THE EYE.

GET GLOWING

Bronzing your skin is easier than ever. A fake tan can make you look thinner and even disguises scars and bruises. Bronzing is an excellent way to get a healthy and natural glow.

DON'T GO TOO DARK

Select a shade that's close to your own skin. On very light skin, a dark self-tanner ends up looking fake.

GET RID OF DEAD SKIN

For an even look, always scrub off patches of dry skin from your knees, heels, and elbows.

APPLYING A GREAT TAN

Apply self-tanner with round, circular motions.

Wash your hands right after applying.

If any stains remain, wipe off with cuticle remover.

FACE TIPS

Start at the center of your forehead, nose, or chin.

Sweep the remainder out to the side of the face up to the hairline.

Go under the jawline and down the neck.

Avoid brows and eye area.

Brush excess over upper lip, earlobes, upper ears, and upper chest.

MAKING EYES

EYEBROWS

They are an important part of the total face. As a rule, they should be one or two shades darker than your hair color.

Don't go crazy with the tweezers, but you don't want to ever leave them unruly.

If you're unsure about what to do, get a stencil kit, or let a professional do it for you.

Always place a little gel on your brows.

SPRAY A TOOTHBRUSH WITH HAIR SPRAY AND BRUSH IT ON YOUR EYEBROWS FOR A SURE HOLD.

If you're too nervous to **TWEEZE**, brush your brows up and snip with a small scissors any hairs that go **ABOVE** the brow.

Choose Thick Brows

If your face is round or heart-shaped.

If your nose is thick or wide.

If you have large or wide set eyes.

If you don't want a lot of maintenance.

Choose Thin Brows

If your face is long and thin.

If your eyes are close- or deep-set.

If your forehead is small.

If you have small features.

Make your **BROWS** look even more dramatic by running a pink or white pencil under the arch.

SHADOW TIPS

Keep your eye shadow from creasing by powdering the eyelid first. Creasing happens when the natural oils in your skin mix with the eye shadow, causing the shadow to collect in the folds of your upper lids.

MASCARA

Black mascara gives the most drama to your eyes. For parties, you can use the same black mascara dipped into a colored shadow. For school or weekends you might prefer a brown mascara or even clear mascara (it doubles as a brow fix). It also may be a better look for you if you're a natural blond or light redhead.

LASHES

It's easy to make any lash look fuller.

- With the pad of your pointer finger, gently pull on the corner of the eye just enough so that skin is smooth and taut.
- Add a thin line of dark powder shadow directly on top of your actual lash line.
- Concentrate your mascara at the base of your lashes with a back and forth motion.
- Then sweep the entire length of the lash once.

197

LINING EYES

It takes practice and a steady hand to apply eyeliner. Here are the steps that will take you there.

- Dust powder over lids if you don't already have eye shadow on.
- If you plan to curl your lashes, do it before lining eyes; otherwise you'll smudge the line.
- Choose the right formula. For a clean, straight line, use a cake or liquid liner.
- To create a soft line, use eyeliner pencil.
- Rest your elbow on a hard surface to steady your hand.
- Start in the middle of the eyelid and draw as close to the lid as possible.
- Draw to the outer end of the eye with a slightly upward turn at the end.

EXTRA CREDIT: SMOKY EYES

To "smoke" your eyes, just apply eye shadow in a similar shade over the liner. If the liner smudges, just clean up with a slightly damped cotton swab.

EYE DRAMA

You can actually change the shape of your eyes with the right makeup techniques. No matter what the size or shape of your eyes, you can make your eyes appear bigger, wider, and more dramatic.

SMALL EYES

Use pale and medium shadows, and stay away from dark colors or dark eyeliner. Apply light shadow over the lids, and a line of medium shadow in the crease.

CLOSE-SET EYES

You can visually separate close-set eyes by using light shimmery shades at the inner corner of each eye. It gives the illusion of more space. Line the outer half of the eye with darker shadow.

DEEP-SET EYES

Deep-set eyes need to come out of hiding. Use a pale shadow all over the lid, and only the lid. Line with a pale liner, and smudge the two together.

WIDE-SET EYES

Wide-set eyes come together by applying dark color at the inner corner of each eye. Apply a lighter shadow at the outer corners.

LIP TRICKS

Open your mouth when applying your lipstick. Use a nude, never a colored lip liner.

Create a full looking mouth by putting a spot of lightweight concealer on the center of your lips after applying lipstick. Then lightly blend it out toward the corners.

WHAT COLOR?

Fair: pale pink, beige or cool red.
Medium: burgundy, caramel, or berry.
Olive/Yellow: brown and plums
Dark: berry, dark red, beige

WHAT KIND?

It's confusing to decide what lipstick to get when there are so many types. Each has its unique qualities and advantages.

Long-wearing: Stays for four to five hours but can also feel dry.
Transfer-resistant: Lasts up to eight hours but can make lips dry and may be hard to remove.
Matte: Lots of color but can look dull.
Cream: Contains lighter waxes but needs reapplication.
Moisturizing: makes lips soft and shiny but doesn't last.
Satin: Lots of oil and moisturizing, but looks darker than actual color.

GET SMOOTH

Before you apply your lipstick, make sure your lips are soft and flake-free.

Brush your teeth, and then gently brush your lips to remove dead skin.

Coat lips with a lip balm and allow it to soak in while you do the rest of your makeup.

BLUSH ✺

HERE'S THE NO. 1 RULE:

The brighter the blush, the less area it should cover. When using a bright shade,

use it only on the apples of your cheeks.

Pink is most flattering to very pale skin.

Medium skin should head to darker pink or light bronze.

Yellow tones will find that berries and plums will counteract sallowness.

Ethnic skin can still wear pink, but with a slightly browner tone.

MAKE SMALL LIPS LOOK FULL

- Stay away from very dark colors.
- Using a neutral lip pencil, draw slightly outside the line.
- Go for a little shimmer. A light-reflective surface can make your lips appear larger.

MAKE FULL LIPS LOOK SMALLER

- Play up your eyes.
- Use a neutral-colored lipstick.
- Don't bother with a lip liner.
- Apply lipstick right from the tube and blend.
- Blot so there's only pigment left on the lips.

ADD SOME CURVES

Using a pencil the color of your lips, draw a V in the bow area of your upper lip, going just above your natural lip line.

FIX IT FAST

Tone down that too bright lipstick by mixing a small dab of foundation with petroleum jelly and patting it over lips.

GOOD TO KNOW

The greasier the lipstick, the more it bleeds. Brown pigments need more oils, so brown lipsticks will probably be greasier.

INSTEAD OF LINER

Get a line around your lips without bothering with lip liner by applying your lipstick with a brush.

TESTING LIPSTICK

You probably think that the correct way to test lipstick is on the back of your hand. But makeup artists know that the true color will come out on your fingertips. The texture and color of the skin on your fingers is more like your lips.

CONTOURING

With the right contouring techniques, it can look like you've lost weight, you've changed the shape of your face, and you've got planes and angles of a top supermodel.

When you try to contour and you do it incorrectly, it ends up looking like you've got streaks of dirt on your face.

MAKE IT EASY

- Choose a color tone. Contouring can help create shadows where they don't normally occur. Go no more than two shades deeper than your natural skin tone. Otherwise it makes your face look strange.
- Apply color by sucking in your cheeks, and with your fingers, feel your cheekbones. Step your fingers down until you feel natural hollows. This is the area where you should concentrate your blush. Roll the brush up to your temples. Don't just sweep it up, or it will look like a line. Lightly rolling will appear more natural.

- Right above your blush, apply a highlighter. Be sure to blend the edges with the blush with your fingers. The look is never to let any lines show on the face.

FACIAL CONTOURING

Long Face

Dust blush on top of your forehead, along your jawline, and under your cheekbones.

Don't go too far down your face, no further than the bottom of your nose.

Square Face

Shade the sides of your jaw and forehead. Sweep over your cheekbones

Heart-Shaped Face

Shade the sides of your forehead, temples, and tip of your chin. Sweep over your cheekbones.

MAKEUP PRO RULES

- **Always apply cream products before powder**
- **Dot dark eye pencil or liner in between lashes to give the appearance of thicker lashes.**

- Shorten your nose with bronzing powder or a darker foundation at the tip.
- Slim your nose by applying a stripe of lighter powder or foundation down the center of your nose.

EXPIRATION DATES

Unlike drugs, expiration dates are not required on cosmetics.

Most dermatologists and opthalmologists I've interviewed recommend the following guidelines for insuring that your cosmetics are safe.

Lipstick....discard after six months

Foundation....discard after one year

Mascara....after three to four months

Blush/powder...one year

Cream...six to eight months

IF THERE IS ANY KIND OF SMELL OR OTHER ODOR COMING FROM ANY BEAUTY PRODUCT, IT'S GONE BAD. THROW IT AWAY IMMEDIATELY.

Chapter 18

CARE AND MAINTENANCE

CLOTHES CARE

Cleaning doesn't have to be done as often as you think. Too frequent cleaning can wear out fabric. Spot clean necklines and underarms and dry clean fabrics only when it's necessary.

To save on **DRY CLEANING**, toss the item into the dryer for ten minutes with a couple of dryer sheets and a washcloth dampened with fragrant soap.

Once you've perspired heavily in an item, it's time to send it to the dry cleaners. Perspiration can discolor clothing if it is allowed to settle in. You will find clothing with "dry clean only" labels that really don't require dry cleaning. If a piece of clothing has a symbol along with a dry clean label, then you really do need to dry clean. These labels are shown when the fabric has been tested. If it doesn't have the symbol, then test a bit of the fabric. It may be washable.

Don't try to wash **WOOL** unless the item states that it is washable. The exception to this rule is **CASHMERE**, which actually softens as it's washed.

Wash cashmere in slightly warm water mixed with a teaspoon of shampoo. Use conditioning shampoo to make your cashmere clothing extra soft.

If an item has a lot of color in it, be aware that even though it might be washable, you'll sacrifice a lot of its color by washing it.

THAT CLOSET CONNECTION

ORGANIZING

- Start by taking everything out of your closet.
- Make four piles:

  Things to keep (that you really feel good in!)

  Things that need work like mending or cleaning

  Things to trade or give away

  Things you aren't sure about

EXTRA CREDIT

If there's a question about throwing something away, at least take it out of your closet. Put it in a box and store it under your bed. Check it in a couple of months. If you've missed it, then put it back into your closet. If it doesn't look fresh and hopeful, it's gone.

- **Arrange clothing by category and subcategory. Long-sleeved blouses, short-sleeved blouses, etc.**

- **Keep things you love and wear a lot in the front of your closet.**
- **After you've reorganized, see what you're missing.**

THROW IT OUT!

- **If you have to lie down, suck in, or fold skin to get it zipped.**
- **If you can't sit, walk, or reach without yanking or pulling.**
- **If it's so short you risk arrest.**

CROWDING

A crowded closet is a guaranteed wrinkle creator. Button up jackets and blouses. Zip zippers and hang pants down from the waist or cuffs. These tricks buy you more room.

NO WIRE HANGERS!

The life of your clothing greatly depends on the type of hanger that you use.

There are hangers made for everything you own.

Padded Hangers

These are made for delicate clothing, like silk blouses.

Jacket/Trouser Hanger

These versatile hangers can put outfits together and hold jackets and coats.

Clamp Hanger

Get a couple to hold skirts and slacks without wrinkling. It also helps to keep creases.

If you do get a **WIRE HANGER** urge, make sure it's coated in plastic.

Make your own **SKIRT HANGER** by adding clothespins to a regular hanger.

Keep clothing from slipping off hangers by wrapping a **RUBBER BAND** around the end of the hanger. The rubber band will "grab" the material and keep the top secure.

QUICK CLOSET TIPS

A bulletin board is great for keeping jewelry in sight. A peg board can hold belts, purses, and long necklaces.

Never store your clothing in plastic bags; they trap moisture and solvent fumes.

Prevent mildew by keeping chalk in your closet. Line up the chalk against the closet baseboard.

DRESS TO GO

Get dressed quickly by organizing your closet with your outfits ready to go.

Drape belts and jewelry over the hanger of the clothes you most often wear them with.

Arrange your clothing in the following way, starting from one end of your closet.

Dress

Pants

Skirts

Long-sleeved tops

Short-sleeved tops

Sleeveless tops/tanks

Arrange clothing according to color.

Hang **LONG** things together so the short items give you an open space on the floor.

To keep your **DRAWERS** organized, used cleaned yogurt cups to hold panty hose. Label the colors for a quick selection.

SHOES

I've seen so many looks spoiled by the wrong shoes, cheap looking shoes (notice I said looking, not costing), or shoes that were scuffed, scratched, or just plain dirty.

The way to keep shoes looking great is to take care of them just like you do your clothing. That would be on a daily or at least on an every other day basis. A cloth here, a bit of polish there, and you're proud to show those tootsies off.

• Choose leather that's soft to the touch, or that you can at least bend a bit.
• Wipe down your shoes with a soft cloth when you come back from bad weather, dust, or just a day of heavy use.

• A small toothbrush is good for wiping off surface dirt.

PATENT LEATHER LOOKS BRAND NEW WHEN YOU CLEAN IT WITH WINDOW CLEANER AND BUFF WITH A CLOTH. CLEAN NON-LEATHER SHOES WITH ANY ALL-PURPOSE SPRAY. BE SURE THE CLEANER DOESN'T CONTAIN BLEACH.

Out of shoe polish? Spray a clean cloth with furniture polish and rub on shoes. Shine with another clean cloth.

Clean suede with a suede-cleaning bar, available at most stores. Get rid of rain spots on suede by rubbing the spots lightly with an emery board.

If shoes get wet, stuff them with newspaper right away after taking them off. This keeps their shape.

Camouflage scuffs and scratches on leather shoes by filling them in with a felt-tip marker in the same color.

DON'T PUT WET SHOES NEAR HEAT

unless you want to shrink them.

BOOTS

Keep leather boots from wrinkling by putting an empty egg carton in each leg.

CLOTHES CARE

Hang heavy clothes by the ribbon loops sewn inside.

Wet garments should be hung on padded hangers. Allow to dry at room temperature, away from heat.

Clean corduroy items by turning them inside out before washing. This will reduce lint and keep the pile from being worn down.

LEATHER

Hang wrinkles out when possible. When you can't, use an iron on a low, rayon setting. Iron the leather inside-out.

Use padded hangers to protect leather's shape.

Never store leather clothing in plastic or nonbreathable bags. Use pillowcases.

Use heavy brown paper bag as a pressing cloth on the right side of the garment. Press down only a second to avoid damage or shine.

Sprinkle cornstarch on oil and grease stains on your leathers. Let it sit overnight.

Then brush away stain with a sponge.

Even with the best cleaners, leather colors may change.

Clean matching leathers together.

SUEDE

Spray a stain preventing silicone before wearing suede for the first time.

Pick up the nap of suede or faux suede by brushing with a soft toothbrush.

Don't store suede in plastic. It promotes mildew.

Always remove suede garments before using hairspray or perfume.

Don't store suede near heat.

JEANS

Wash dark jeans in cold water in the sink. Hang them to drip dry, and they'll slowly develop an antique finish in all the right places.

Machine wash jeans with detergent and ½ cup of table salt before wearing to soften the denim.

To **PREVENT** your skirt from clinging to your hose, rinse the hose in water mixed with a teaspoon or two of hair conditioner before you wear them.

STAIN GUIDELINES

- Treat a stain as soon as possible to keep it from setting in.

- Try to keep the garment moist until you can wash it.
- Don't rub a wet stain.
- Brush off a dried stain before trying to wash it.
- Test cleaner on a hidden seam or hem.
- Read care labels.
- Work stain from the outside toward the center.
- Follow instructions on the cleaning bottles.
- Avoid using very hot water. It will set most stains.
- Always use cleaners in a well-ventilated area.

BLOOD

Sponge with cool water and rinse clear.

Sponge with hydrogen peroxide if the blood has dried. Allow to bubble. Then rinse.

CHOCOLATE

Stretch fabric over a bowl and secure with a rubber band. Sprinkle Borax over the stain, then pour very hot water over it in a circle. Start at the outer edge and end in the center. Wash as usual.

COFFEE/TEA

Pour boiling water on the stain and wash with soap. Treat remaining stain with baking soda.

DIRT

Add a can of cola in washer along with detergent.

GRASS

Sponge with two teaspoons cold water mixed with one teaspoon rubbing alcohol. Rinse and launder.

GREASE

Rub in petroleum jelly. Rub off excess. Then wash in warm, soapy water.

GUM

Dab with ice to harden, then scrape away as much as possible.

INK

Saturate the stain with hair spray. Place a towel under the stain, and blot. Launder as usual.

KETCHUP

Soak in a paste made with laundry detergent and a small amount of water. Apply white vinegar to heavily stained areas.

LIPSTICK

Rub the stain with petroleum jelly before washing.

MAKEUP

Try to pick up as much as possible with a baby wipe. Then launder as usual.

MILDEW

To get rid of mildew stains, sponge the stained areas with lemon juice. Then put the item in the sun.

MUSTARD

Use a commercial spot remover or rug cleaner.

PAINT

Apply paint thinner. Rinse with cool water and wash as usual.

PERSPIRATION

Add four tablespoons salt to one quart of hot water. Sponge fabric.

Separate laundry by WEIGHT as well as color for less harm to delicate fabrics.

Hang wet pants by the LEGS, not the waist, for less wrinkling.

SWEAT STAINS

Remove yellow stains from under arms of your favorite white tops by soaking in a mixture of ¼ cup non-chlorine bleach mixed with two gallons of warm water for two hours before washing.

EXTRA CREDIT
Brighten whites by using a powder fabric whitener along with your regular detergent. Place an old pair of PANTY HOSE in the dryer with dark items. The hose attracts the lint, leaving everything else lint-free!

ACCESSORY CARE

Clean jewelry with denture cleanser.

Clean handbags with a toothbrush dipped in a mixture of ½ cup powder detergent mixed with ½ cup of water.

Keep buttons from disintegrating by applying clear nail polish over the buttons and the threads. It will harden the threads and "glue" them to the button.

Use an old lipstick tube to create a portable sewing kit. Clean out the tube and pop in a cotton ball. Stick threaded needles into the cotton ball. Stick the cap on and carry it with you.

To keep a loose **ZIPPER** from falling down, mist the teeth of the zipper with hair spray. Strong tape can remove **LINT**, seal bottles, and even repair a purse temporarily.

Put a thin coat of clear **NAIL POLISH** on inexpensive jewelry to keep your skin from turning green.

Protect your straw hats and bags by spray-painting them with clear varnish to keep the straw from splitting. It also keeps them from getting dusty.

Keep **COSMETIC** and perfume labels clear by coating them with clear nail polish. The labels can fade over time or smear if they get wet.

CARE AND MAINTENANCE SUPPLIES

Chamois to soak up spots

Toothbrush for tough stains

Double-sided tape for quick hem fixes

Emery board to clean suede

Sewing supplies

Garment bags: use them for out of season and special occasion clothes

Clothes brush: use a wire brush for most fabrics

Lint brush

Iron/ironing board

Silicone spray

Use self-stick tape to pick up lint, hair, and to refresh Velcro.

WATERPROOF YOUR KEYS

BEFORE HEADING TO THE BEACH, SPIKE A HOLE THROUGH A LARGE CORK AND THREAD YOUR KEY RING THOUGH IT. THE CORK WILL KEEP KEYS FLOATING IN CASE THEY ACCIDENTALLY FALL INTO THE WATER. PLUS, THEY MAKE A COOL SUMMER ACCESSORY.

LINGERIE CARE

Hand wash in mild dishwashing detergent or soap detergent. Roll in a towel to blot. Air dry.

Only machine wash in a mesh bag or pillowcase. Simply tie a knot at the top of the pillowcase and close with a safety pin.

Rotate your lingerie. Wear Lycra pieces only once every four to five days so they have time to snap back into shape.

Hand wash LINGERIE with stretch fabric in cool water to retain its elasticity. Never put it in the dryer. Hang or lay flat to dry.

SWEATER CARE

Fold sweaters, unless you want to lengthen them.

Use a baby's hairbrush to remove hairs, lint, etc.

Don't store a sweater in a plastic bag. Natural fabrics need to "breathe."

To keep sweaters from losing their shape after washing, place the sweater unwashed on a sheet of plain paper and trace it with a pencil. After washing, place the sweater on the paper and pin it in place to reshape.

A QUICK FIX FOR A FALLEN HEM... DOUBLE-SIDED TAPE. LOOK FOR 3M BRAND, THE STRONGEST.

217

WHAT DO THOSE LABELS MEAN?

It's important to read labels so that you can properly take care of your clothes, getting the most out of them.

Permanent Press

You can machine wash and machine dry this garment and it won't need ironing.

Make sure you don't overdry, and that you take the garment out as soon the dryer cycle ends.

Pre-Shrunk

It shouldn't shrink after washing.

Release

This means that the fabric has been treated so that soil can be more easily washed.

Stain and Spot Resistant

The fabric has a finish that water and oil can't penetrate.

LOCKER ORGANIZATION

Extend the care and organization of your closet at home to the one you have at school. Use storage tins or yogurt cups to hold pens, pencils, and personal stuff.

Tack on adhesive hooks to save space.

MUST HAVES

Mints
Mirror (for quick peeks in between classes)
Hanging mesh bag for hanging books
Emery boards
Baby wipes for post gym clean ups
Hairbrush

IF YOU HAVE ROOM

Battery operated curling iron
Hair spritzer
Concealer
Air freshener

Chapter 19

SPECIAL EVENTS

For any special event, you still want to look like you, only better. You want to shine.

Whether you're going to a prom, a wedding, or just a night out with friends, wear something that makes you feel gorgeous while being totally comfortable. It's the only way to attend any event.

TRY, TRY, TRY

When you're searching for that perfect dress don't settle on the first one you see. The perfect look may not be evident on the hanger. But you'll know it's the one the second you put it on.

WHAT TO LOOK FOR

LENGTH

Although this is a personal decision there are guidelines.

Full length just touches the floor and is for the most formal of occasions.

Ankle length gowns actually stop at the ankle and are easier to walk in than full length.

Tea length stops at mid-calf and would be more appropriate for a semi-formal occasion.

Street length dresses and minis are what to wear to less formal events like dance parties.

SLEEVES

Consider the weather and the conditions when picking out your sleeve length.

• Fitted sleeves from shoulder to wrist are best for winter events.

• Cap sleeves just cover the top of the shoulders

and really show off well-toned arms.

- Dropped sleeves can be short or long and make a dress look sophisticated.
- Petal sleeves look like flower petals, perfect for a traditional event.
- Sleeveless dresses can be worn with long gloves in the winter.

Bring along a CAMERA when selecting your special occasion dress. Have a friend take pictures of you in each dress. You'll be able to develop the pictures and look at yourself in each dress before you make your decision.

VINTAGE

Here's the great thing about shopping for your special event in a thrift shop: there won't be five other girls at your prom wearing the same dress.

TAKING DAY INTO NIGHT

Dress up slacks with strappy heels.

Change your opaques to fishnets or sheer stockings.

Change your belt to rhinestone, glitter, gold, or anything sparkly.

HOW TO WEAR SEQUINS

To avoid looking like a stripper when wearing anything with sequins, stick to one embellished piece. Wear it with something simple. For instance, wear a sequin top with black pants.

Skip the jewelry when wearing anything sequined.

MAKING UP
LIGHT UP

Matte is for day. Your makeup should be as bright as the lights you'll be under.

Dip a wet brush in a bright eye shadow and use it to line eyes. This gives an intensity to the color, and it dries for longer wear.

KEEP YOUR MAKEUP GOING

Keep lips on all night by applying shimmery eye shadow on top of your lipstick.

Apply in the middle of upper and lower lip and spread out.

Brighten your shadow by brushing on a layer of sheer white shadow first.

Finish eyes and lips before adding blush so you can see how much you need to balance your look.

THE EVENING BAG

Even the smallest bag has room for these essentials.

Breath mints

Pressed powder

Lipstick

Small mirror

Comb or retractable brush

MAKE YOUR OWN EVENING BAG

Save money and make a statement by making your own prom or evening bag. It's easy and fun! Here's what you'll need.

A half-yard of fabric (use an upholstery fabric or velvet)
One yard ribbon (for the strap)
Decorations/appliqué
Matching thread
Sewing needle
Scissors
Cardboard
Straight pins
Large safety pin

Cut the cardboard into an 8" x 9" long rectangle.
Lay your fabric out flat and folded in half.
Place your cardboard pattern on top of the fabric.
Cut the fabric, using the edges of the pattern as a guide.
Fold over each side of the fabric to create a ½ inch hem.
Use pins to secure the hem in place.
Sew the entire length of hem using a running stitch.
Create a tunnel wide enough for the ribbon and sew both sides.
Sew the bottom of the bag, closing up the bottom.
Add your details.

WHAT TO EAT BEFORE THE BIG EVENT

Here's how to make sure your dress fits and you look fabulous for that special evening. It's what the models do before a big runway show.

- Cut down on salt the day before.
- Avoid sugar
- Drink a lot of water
- Drink grapefruit juice as a natural debloater.

Hair Occasions

CURLS are always in style for special events.

So are **UP DOS**—just be sure they don't make you look like you're trying too hard.

Twist up your hair loosely and **PIN** it in place, leaving ends loose. Complete the look by leaving some pieces out around your **FACE**.

Chapter 20

COLLEGE SECRETS

WHAT TO TAKE

CHECK WITH YOUR COLLEGE FIRST

Although it's tempting to go shopping first, you need to check with the school you'll be attending. Most colleges and universities have rules about what students can and cannot bring with them.

Of course, before you fill this list, it would be a good idea to contact your roommate so that you don't duplicate efforts.

BASICS FOR YOUR ROOM

A computer
A TV (with a VCR/DVD) if possible
An alarm clock/radio
A marker board for the door so you'll
    know who has been by
Posters
2 mirrors (one a magnifying mirror)

2 sheet sets
Comforter and blanket
2 pillows
Egg cot and mattress pad
Laundry detergent and dryer sheets
Laundry basket and laundry bag
Coins for the laundry machines
CD player and CDs
An iron
Phone with an answering machine
Storage box
Lamp

FOR YOUR OWN PERSONAL USE

Hair dryer, curling iron/flat iron
Comfortable clothing
Dress up clothing
Comfortable shoes/dress shoes
Sneakers
Backpack
Tissues
Shampoo, deodorant, toothbrush/paste, etc.

NICE TO HAVE

Your high school yearbook. It's fun to show your new friends, and it will help you to get over feeling lonely and homesick.

Miniature refrigerator. This saves you from losing snacks in the common room, and allows you to have a few things handy.

Inline skates

Bike

Photos of your family, friends, and pets

Umbrella

Stain remover

First-Aid kit

Duffle bag

Flip Flops

Lots of tape

Instead of a regular **COTTON** pillowcase, pack a satin pillowslip. They cost no more than most regular cases, and will keep you from waking up with **BED HEAD**. Plus, it will keep you from waking up with that sleep line on your face.

There's never **ENOUGH SPACE** to store your stuff, so store your extra blankets between your mattress and box spring. This way, they won't take up closet space and they'll make your mattress more comfortable.

HOW TO GET ENOUGH SLEEP

New strange place, odd noises, how's a girl going to get her beauty sleep? Follow the advice of long-time dorm dwellers.

CHILL OUT

You may sleep more soundly in a cooler room. If you have air conditioning that is centrally controlled, open the window a crack.

TAKE A BATH OR WARM SHOWER

You'll raise your body temperature while you're in, and then you'll get a major temperature drop. This tells the body it's ready to sleep.

DISTRACT YOURSELF

Worrying about not sleeping can cause insomnia. Play some soothing music, or just let your mind wander. Reading something light (like a fashion magazine) also will help.

HOW TO STAY HEALTHY

What do you do to stay healthy when your roommate and everyone else in your dorm are fighting colds and flu? When everyone else is sick and those germs are just waiting to come your way, you need a little strategy.

DON'T TOUCH!

It seems obvious to avoid touching sick people, but also try not to touch yourself, until you've washed your hands anyway. Studies have shown that we touch our hands to our eyes every three hours.

KEEP YOUR DISTANCE

If you find yourself near a person who's coughing and sneezing, try to keep a few feet away.

SOAP UP

You know that you should wash your hands before eating, but you also need to do it before drinking. If you open a bottle or touch a glass with dirty hands, not only have you contaminated your drink, you've contaminated yourself.

GET SOME AIR

Crack your window open to ventilate your space and get rid of airborne toxins.

DON'T SHARE TOWELS

Have a separate towel for your roommate, and wash your own after two uses.

SCENT YOUR PILLOW

Take a little eucalyptus oil and sprinkle your pillow with it before turning in. The scent will protect your nose and lungs from virus and bacteria.

HOW TO AVOID THE FRESHMAN FIFTEEN

With unlimited meal plans and more variety than you could have ever imagined, it's not only mind-blowing, but thigh-growing. You don't have to get a new wardrobe when you go home for the holidays if you just take a few smart steps.

JUST BECAUSE IT'S "ALL YOU CAN EAT" DOESN'T MEAN YOU HAVE TO EAT IT ALL

One trip in line is all you should make. Fill half your plate with salad or veggies. Use your fist to figure out what you need for an entrée, and allow yourself two thumbfuls of bread or other carbs.

GET UP FOR BREAKFAST

Although it doesn't seem like it's worth it, it is. Even if you can't eat in the cafeteria, stop by. Pick up a box of cereal and a banana. It will keep your energy up and will keep your power going until the afternoon.

AVOID PIG OUT PARTIES

Let your pals eat as much as they want. You deal the cards, show the pictures, and sip water or diet soda. Chances are, your friends will be so busy chowing down, they won't even notice.

BE SAVVY AT THE SALAD BAR

You may think that you're eating healthy, but if you use a high-fat dressing, croutons, and bacon or grated cheese, then the pounds will start piling on. Although the salad bar can create a great low-fat meal, you have to know what to choose.

KEEP IT OUT OF SIGHT

Don't keep big bags of munchies in your room. Bring only enough from the cafeteria to tide you over to the next day. An apple or a few raisins is all you need to study by.

LEAVE THESE AT HOME

- The Clean Plate Club
- Eating fast
- Eating lots of bread
- Salting your food before tasting it. It makes you bloated, and it's not necessary.
- High calorie drinks

WHETHER IT'S LEMONADE OR KOOL-AID, YOU DON'T WANT TO USE UP YOUR CALORIES WITH LESS THAN NUTRITIOUS DRINKING.

BEATING FATIGUE

No matter what your schedule, with the hectic pace of college life, you're bound to suffer from fatigue from time to time, especially around exam time.

Although coffee seems like the perfect pick up, your body processes the caffeine too quickly. The same goes for sugar. You may feel an immediate feeling of energy, but it doesn't last.

HERE'S WHAT TO DO.

- Drink enough water. You need to stay hydrated to stay energized.
- Keep some peanut butter around. It's packed with protein.
- Yogurt is a great snack, but try to find the low-fat kind.
- Complex carbohydrates fuel your body. Cereal with at least six grams of fiber makes a quick low-calorie snack.
- Dried fruit and nuts are great study snacks. Keep trail mix with you.

231

Chapter 21

QUICK FIXES

Got a beauty emergency? Whether it's a time crunch, you're out of product, or something has "popped" up, you'll love this chapter.

SKIN SOLUTIONS

ACNE

This is the No. 1 beauty emergency. Deal with them on the "spot."

If the bump seems really red or swollen, apply an ice cube to reduce signs of inflammation.

To reduce redness, use an eye redness reliever or hydrocortisone. Hemorrhoid cream also works.

Dab on calamine lotion. It dries up and absorbs excess oil.

Mix one tablespoon of lemon juice and one tablespoon cornstarch. Pat the paste on the blemish and let dry.

SHAVING NICKS

Moisten a dry tea bag with cold water and place it on the cut to stop the bleeding.

INSECT BITES

Mix one part meat tenderizer to four parts water and apply to the bite.

SUNBURN

Chill a spray bottle of vinegar in the fridge, and then spray it on your burn.

Rub a peeled cucumber on the sunburn.

Pop an anti-inflammatory like ibuprofen.

Rub aloe vera gel on the burn.

POWDER OVERLOAD

Spritz your face with water and blot with a tissue for more natural coverage.

Take a large, fluffy brush and go over your face in circles.

QUICK GLOW FOR SALLOW SKIN

Three minutes: Splash your face with as much cold water as you can handle about ten times. This gets blood flowing and invigorates skin.

Two minutes: Tap all over your face (lightly slapping yourself) until you feel your face tingle.

One minute: Apply bronzing or shimmer powder on your forehead, cheeks, and chin.

Thirty seconds: Drop your head to the floor. This revs up circulation and puts color in your cheeks.

RED NOSE

Apply allergy drops with a cotton swab. Spread a mixture of green eye shadow and concealer to color correct.

EYES

PUFFY EYES

Run teaspoons under cold water, and place them under your eyes for a few seconds. Then close your eyes and gently roll and massage the rounded side of the spoon over the eye area.

DARK CIRCLES

Apply sliced potatoes under the eye and lie down for five minutes, allowing the juices to seep in. Treat with the contents of a vitamin K capsule.

Mix bright blue shadow with facial moisturizer and dab it under your eyes.

HEAVY EYELINER

Go over the line with a light-colored eye shadow to soften the look.

SMASHED EYE SHADOW

Store it in a small clean plastic or glass container and use it as a loose shadow.

LIPS

CHAPPED/DRY LIPS

Press tape against chapped lips and peel off dead skin cells.

SMEARED LIPSTICK

1) Dip a cotton swab in eye makeup remover.
2) Apply foundation with a cotton swab to clean up the look.

MUSTACHE MENDING

If you waxed your upper lip and now it's pink and swollen, dip a washcloth in cold milk and press it to the area. This will soothe the skin and lessen the inflammation.

BROKEN LIPSTICK

Put broken lipstick back together by heating the broken piece with a match until soft. Then sit it back on the tube, waiting five minutes before rolling it down the tube.

Put it in the freezer for ten minutes to weld it together.

HAIR EMERGENCIES

GREASIES

Blot your scalp with a baby wipe, followed by a tissue that's been pulled apart.

FRIZZIES

Mix equal amounts of conditioner and gel in your palms and run it over your hair.

The gel will hold your style while the conditioner will control the frizz.

Pat moisturizer lightly over the top layer of hair.

NO TIME TO TOUCH UP ROOTS

Use colored sidewalk chalk.
Pat on powdered eye shadow.

NO TIME TO SHAMPOO

Pull hair into a low ponytail, leaving a few strands loose in front. Wash the strands and allow to dry. The strands will fake clean hair.

Shake a little cornstarch on your roots and brush through.

HAIR BUILD-UP

Get rid of product build-up and bring hair back to life by adding a tablespoon of baking soda with two tablespoons of shampoo.

QUICK DREADS

Divide your hair into one-inch sections and coat each with styling wax. Twist tightly around your finger. Repeat until your entire head is complete.

COILS

Wet hair and saturate with gel. Separate hair into one-inch sections and wrap tightly around a straw. Secure at the root to keep straws in place. Allow hair to dry or blow dry on the lowest setting. Slip out straws.

QUICK SHINE

After shampooing and conditioning gently stroke hair from roots to ends with an ice cube. The cold seals the hair shaft, so it reflects light better.

Run a small amount of baby oil through your hair.

NO TIME TO BLOW DRY

Blow dry only the hair on top of your head, above the ears. It's what frames your face and what people see first.

BLOW DRYER BURN OUT

Apply a few drops of castor oil with a grooming cream once hair is dry.

QUICK BANG TRIM

You can trim your own bangs. Start with dry bangs. Use the top half inch of a pair of small scissors with the blades angled upward, not across. Snip small pieces from side to side at least fifteen to twenty times.

TOO MUCH HAIR COLOR

If your hair came out too dark, shampoo with a mild dishwashing liquid. It will lift away from of the color pigment.

Shampoo with a dandruff shampoo, lathering twice.

TOO MUCH HAIR PRODUCT

Blot a witch hazel–soaked cotton ball over excess product to break down the product. Continue styling.

FAKE AN UP DO

Use a ponytail holder that looks like braided hair. Pull hair back into a low ponytail and twist into a bun. Secure with an elastic band and cover with holder.

EMERGENCY HAIR MOUSSE

Use a small amount of shaving cream in a fix. (not shaving gel).

CHLORINE-COLORED HAIR

Rinse with apple cider vinegar, followed by club soda.

BAD HAIRCUT

Slick back with gel.
Experiment with barrettes and headbands.

NAIL EMERGENCIES

YELLOW NAILS

Soak your nails in ¼ cup bleach mixed with ½ cup water.

NO TIME FOR A MANICURE

Pass up the polish and give nails a quick buff with a nail file. They'll have smoothness and shine, and you won't have to wait for them to dry.

Apply **CLEAR LIP BALM** to nails for a polished look.

NOT QUITE DRY

Coat wet nails with cuticle oil and cover your nails with plastic wrap.

SMUDGE

Moisten the pad of your finger with polish remover and tap lightly to smooth it out.

CHIPPED POLISH

Moisten your finger with polish remover and quickly swipe over the chipped area to smooth out the edges.

BROKEN NAIL

If the break isn't too low, carefully cut the nail, file it, and trim the other nails so that they're equal.

For a big break (into the nail bed), apply a couple of drops of nail glue to the surface of the nail. Let set and hold the break in place for about a minute. Reapply glue and cover the nail with a piece of tea bag or tissue. Let dry, and then buff excess off.

NAIL BUBBLES

Go over the bubbles with a topcoat.

EMERGENCY NAIL POLISH REMOVERS

- Use insect repellent (like "Off") when you need to remove your nail polish and there's none to be found.
- Apply topcoat and rub off with a tissue.

No Time for Makeup

APPLY A LITTLE BRONZER TO EYES, LIPS, AND CHEEKS.

USE MASCARA IN PLACE OF LINER AND SHADOW. A CURLING MASCARA WILL ELIMINATE ANOTHER STEP.

STICK TO GLOSS AND SHEER LIPSTICKS. THEY CAN BE APPLIED QUICKLY WITHOUT SMUDGING.

CLOTHING EMERGENCIES

QUICK LINT REMOVER

Use sticky labels. It works faster than a skinny strip of tape.

BUTTON POPS

Strip the paper off a storage bag tie and use the metal to thread through the buttonhole.

Twist it at the back to stay put.

Grab some dental floss and pass it through the hole where the button fell off, and through the buttonhole. Tie the ends together.

If you RUN OUT of fabric softener, put a couple of drops hair conditioner on a washcloth and toss it in with the clothes.

PERSONAL EMERGENCIES

STOP HUNGER QUICKLY

Using a circular motion, rub the area between your upper lip and nose with your index finger for ten seconds. This fools the brain into signaling the stomach that it's satisfied

GET A FLAT TUMMY

Keep away from carbonated beverages, even fizzy water, which can introduce air into the stomach.

Don't chew gum or sip from a straw because you'll swallow air.

Keep gas away by staying away from beans, cauliflower, peppers, and onions.

PROBLEMS & SOLUTIONS

YOU'RE NOT ALONE

Don't worry. For every beauty problem, there's a beauty solution. Chances are, someone else has dealt with your problem, and we've come up with a great fix.

MY MAKEUP DOESN'T LAST.

Use less moisturizer.

Use an oil-free foundation.

Apply powder over eyes.

Use eye and cheek stain rather than powder versions. They last longer.

I DON'T KNOW HOW TO APPLY MAKEUP UNDER MY GLASSES.

Eyes should be brighter under glasses.

If you're nearsighted, apply a dark shadow on your lids, a light one on the brow bone, and mascara.

If you're farsighted, use light shades and mascara.

MY LIPS NOT ONLY CHAP, THEY EVEN SPLIT.

Prevent them by applying a balm when sleeping. Cracks often occur because of sleeping in dry air. Treat them by applying an antibiotic like Neosporin. You also might want to use a humidifier.

MY LASHES KEEP FALLING OUT.

Avoid rubbing your eyelids.

Use a warm spoon over your eyes to curl your lashes.

Use a mascara with conditioning ingredients.

I WANT TO APPEAR LIKE I HAVE LONGER LEGS.

Create the illusion of a longer leg with a straight legged, high-waisted pant. Keep details on the pant to a minimum.

HOW DO I GET BETTER POSTURE?

Practice these three easy exercises.

- Stand facing a mirror, feet parallel and shoulder width apart. Pull your navel in towards your spine without bending your back. Gently tense your bottom muscles. Square your shoulders without lifting your lower ribs.
- On your hands and knees, relax your tummy and slowly pull your navel and muscle below it up towards your spine. Hold for ten seconds and gently release.
- Put your hands on your buttocks and clench your muscles, then slowly release. Practice this when you're standing (in private).

HOW DO I GROW OUT MY BANGS?

Hide them with a side part coated with enough gel to create spikes.

Use barrettes to disguise length and to flow with the rest of your hair.

WHEN DO I THROW MY COSMETICS OUT?

Your makeup will show definite signs when its time has run out.

Mascara will clump, flake, or start to smell.
Eyeliner will liquefy or give off a strange odor.
Lipstick will streak or the surface will oil up.
Foundation will turn yellow or separate.
Powders will break easily or change color.

Chapter 22

TEENS AND SURGERY

It's a fact of life. Our looks matter, and more and more teens are looking to better themselves. I want you to know as much as possible about plastic surgery so that you can think about it, talk it over with your parents, and be realistic in your expectations.

I've gone right to the source, a plastic surgeon who has worked with teens. Dr. Sheldon Sevinor of Boston, Massachusetts, is one of the nation's pre-eminent plastic surgeons. He has appeared on *The Oprah Winfrey Show* and *Sally Jesse Raphael*, and has contributed to many national newspapers and publications. He is known for his candid and caring manner. What better resource for this important and ever growing field?

Diane: Dr. Sevinor, how common is surgery for teens?

Dr. Sevinor: Cosmetic surgery for people aged eighteen and younger represents about 3 percent of the total number of cosmetic procedures performed in the United States each year.

Diane: What are the usual reasons?

Dr. Sevinor: The reason to have cosmetic surgery involves body image.

Diane: What are the most common operations?

Dr. Sevinor: The most common operations performed on teens include reduction mammoplasty (breast reduction), rhinoplasty (nose reshaping), otoplasty (ear reshaping), correction of breast asymmetry (uneven breasts), gynecomastia (enlarged male breasts), and chin augmentation.

Diane: How is your approach with a teen different from other patients?

Dr. Sevinor: There is a great deal of psychology involved in cosmetic surgery, and it is very important that the plastic surgeon have a meaningful communication with the patient. This type of surgery is highly personal, and it is imperative that the plastic surgeon understands why a teenager wants to change some aspect of her appearance, and to ascertain whether or not those reasons are valid.

Diane: What do you tell the patient who comes to you in regards to her looks?

Dr. Sevinor: The teenager must be realistic as to expectations. As plastic surgeons, we attempt improvement, but can never reach perfection. There are no guarantees made as to the results that may be obtained, nor are there any guarantees made against unfavorable results. If the patient is unrealistic as to the expectations of what cosmetic surgery can accomplish, then she will never be happy. And each plastic surgeon must be a keen psychologist.

Diane: How do you evaluate a teen's readiness?

Dr. Sevinor: It is important to evaluate both the teenager's physical and emotional maturity. Each case is given individual, careful evaluation. The process begins with a consultation. During this consultation the plastic surgeon must ask and evaluate two key concerns:

1.) Did the teenage patient have the desire for a long period of time to seek the advice of a plastic surgeon regarding some aspect of their appearance that has bothered her? 2.) It is imperative that it is the teenager, rather than her parents, desire to change some aspect of her appearance for the right reasons. Although it is important to have parental support from an emotional standpoint, it is the patient that ultimately needs to evaluate her own emotional and physical appearance. The decision to seek consultation with the plastic surgeon should not be a whim, rather a thought process that has taken place over a long period of time.

Diane: Do you see the teen and parents together?

Dr. Sevinor: In my practice, I like to see the teenager privately without the parent in the consultation room initially so that I can evaluate whether it is the teen or it is the parent who is pushing for a cosmetic surgical procedure. I've had requests that the parent come into the room many times when a teenager will come to me, and her parents will tell me how much more attractive their child might look if she had a nose reshaping procedure. However, when I evaluate the desire for the procedure by the teenager it appears that she is really happy with the way she looks, and she is not bothered by the appearance of her nose. I would never operate on a teenager under those circumstances.

Diane: What do you look for?

Dr. Sevinor: Does a teenager have realistic expectations as to what we can accomplish with cosmetic surgery? Young patients must understand the benefits and risk and limitations of cosmetic surgery. An unrealistic patient in terms of expectation will never be happy.

Diane: What else is important?

Dr. Sevinor: Is the teenager mature both physically and emotionally? The teen must be emotionally stable and not be clinically depressed or have any other mental illness.

Diane: What if they mention a celebrity?

Dr. Sevinor: Cosmetic surgery is performed to improve the patient's appearance, self-image, and self-esteem. Most of my patients want to be a better version of themselves rather than looking like someone else. The reason to have plastic surgery involves body image, which is the subjective perception of the body as it is seen through the mind's eye. Body image development changes as we age, it is a very sensitive time as the teenager undergoes major changes in his or her physical appearance. It is a time of increased vulnerability to the opinion of their peers. A major key to achieving success with cosmetic surgery is appropriate patient selection. The realistic, highly motivated teenager may be an appropriate candidate for cosmetic surgery, but the teen with psychopathology will not be an appropriate candidate.

Diane: Thank you, Dr. Sevinor, and now because I know you for your candor, let's talk about breast augmentation and liposuction. How do you feel about these procedures?

Dr. Sevinor: In regard to these two procedures, I feel that there is a great deal of controversy. It is my personal opinion that a teenager should not undergo breast augmentation or liposuction procedures until they are more mature both physically and emotionally. In rare cases where there is significant physical deformity, or with a teenager with almost no breast development on one side, I would consider breast augmentation. Even in that situation, the patient would have to meet specific criteria.

When I see a patient who desires liposuction, I inform her that liposuction is not a "quick fix." It is not a method for dieting. It is a serious procedure, and is generally not appropriate for the teen. I encourage teenagers to eat nutritiously, and to exercise appropriately, sometimes with a trainer.

COMMON COSMETIC PLASTIC SURGERY PROCEDURES FOR TEENS

RHINOPLASTY

This cosmetic surgery procedure is done to reshape the nose and make it appear more attractive. Generally this is not performed until the nose reaches its adult size, about aged fifteen or sixteen in girls, and about aged sixteen or seventeen in boys.

The procedure is done under general anesthesia with one night in the hospital. A splint and packing of the nose is used for one week and then a special tape remains on the nose for another week. Patients are able to return to school after two weeks.

BREAST REDUCTION

This procedure is done to reduce very large, pendulous breasts that can cause physical and psychological problems. Many teenage patients complain about pain in the back, chest, shoulders, and neck. There is often a great deal of psychological trauma in terms of how these patients are viewed by their peers. Surgery is done when breast growth stops, usually at age seventeen to eighteen. Surgery is done under general anesthesia with one night in the hospital, and the recovery usually takes two weeks.

OTOPLASTY

Cosmetic surgery to correct protruding ears. The procedure is done by recontouring the cartilage of the ears and essentially pinning them back. The procedure is done any time after age five when the ears are 95 percent full size. The best time to have this done is at age five because many of these children are subjected to harsh comments by their classmates. This is done under general anesthesia or local anesthesia, and is usually done on an outpatient basis. Recovery takes about one to two weeks.

CORRECTION OF GYNECOMASTIA

This is done to correct large breasts in boys, many of whom are embarrassed to remove their T-shirts in public. Sometimes this is a hereditary condition. Sometimes this condition will disappear on its own. Severe excess breast tissue can be removed from teenagers at age eighteen.

CORRECTION OF BREAST ASYMMETRY

This is done when one breast is much larger in size than the other; in fact, some teenagers have no breast development at all in one side. This operation corrects discrepancy by either reducing the larger breast, augmenting the smaller breast, or both. This condition can be psychologically devastating for a young teenager. It can be done on a teen at age sixteen or older, depending on her physical and emotional maturity. The procedure is done under general anesthesia, with one night in the hospital, and recovery is about two weeks.

CHIN AUGMENTATION

This is a cosmetic surgery procedure to improve a receding chin. Chin implants are inserted in order to augment the chin and make it appear more attractive. This is done for both female and male patients after the age of fifteen. The procedure can be done under local or general anesthesia, and the patients can return home on the same day. The recovery period is usually one to two weeks. The procedure is often done at the same time as nose reshaping (rhinoplasty).

WAYS TO FIND A GOOD PLASTIC SURGEON

GET RECOMMENDATIONS

Talk to friends and physicians you trust. Call the American Society of Plastic Surgeons at 800-635-0635.

ASK HOW MANY TIMES A DOCTOR HAS DONE THE PROCEDURE YOU ARE LOOKING FOR

An experienced doctor may be able to master a new technique after doing it a few times, but a new doctor may need more experience.

CHECK CLAIMS

No reputable cosmetic surgeon will give somebody a celebrity nose, breasts, or chin. Don't go in carrying a photo of Sharon Stone's nose or wanting Gwyneth Paltrow's cheekbones. Most operations are performed according to the shape of the patient's own face, and some things are not physically possible to change.

FINAL WORDS AND BEST WISHES

Your teens are the years of so many things, and **BEAUTY HAS A RIGHT TO BE THERE**. It is my hope that you incorporate beauty into **WHATEVER** you do. **ADMIRE** the beauty you see in others as you **CAPTURE THE BEAUTY WITHIN YOURSELF**.

Bring beauty along wherever you go. Know that you had fun with it, it **LIFTED YOUR SPIRITS**, and it didn't hurt you or anyone else. Yes, I've seen it misused, but when it's done with **PURE INTENTIONS** it can **MAKE THE WORLD A LITTLE NICER**.

I've tried to include everything I think you should know about **LOOKING AND FEELING GOOD** during your teen years.

These tips are meant to make your life easier, not more complicated. Pick this book up whenever you need it. **BEING A TEEN HAS NEVER LOOKED SO COOL.**

SITES & RESOURCES

Here are some sites I've come across that I thought you might enjoy.

SHOPPING ADVICE SITES

www.fashionmall.com
www.focusonstyle.com
www.TheTrendReport.com
www.Saleshound.com
www.salesmountain.com
www.inshop.com
www.internetmall.com

DESIGNER SITES

www.chanel.com
www.ArmaniExchange.com
www.donnakaran.com

SHOPPING SITES

www.GUESS.com
www.gap.com
www.bluefly.com

www.girlshop.com
www.bestpromdresses.com
www.turnstylz.com

FASHION SITES

www.firstview.com

FREE STUFF

www.TeenFreeway.com

FUN SITES

www.astrologyfashion.com
www.quackwatch.com

BEAUTY SITES

www.Beautycare.com
www.Emakemeup.com
www.Profaces.com
www.beautyofasite.com
www.beautyscene.com

SKIN ADVICE

www.dermadoctor.com

HAIR SITES

www.Robertcraig.com

www.Salonweb.com

www.yoursalon.com

JUST FOR TEENS

www.Teenrefuge.com

FOOD & FITNESS SITES

www.ediets.com

www.whymilk.com

BODY/HEALTH INFORMATION

www.tampax.com

PRODUCT REVIEWS

www.Epinions.com

SWIMSUIT HELP

www.jantzenswim.com

HELP HOTLINES

Suicide & Crisis Hotline: 800-999-9999

National Suicide Prevention: 800-SUICIDE

SAFE (Self-Abuse Finally Ends): 800-Dont Cut

Teen Line: 800-522-8336

American Dietetic Association: 800-366-1655

American Anorexia/Bulemia Association Inc.: 212-501-8351

National Association of Anorexia and Associated Disorders: 847-831-3438

INDEX

ABOUT THE AUTHOR

DIANE IRONS began her highly successful career as a model at age thirteen, then transferred her skills and expertise to training other up-and-coming models as well as directing major photo shoots and runway shows. She continues to do so today while sharing her secrets with audiences throughout the world. As a leading force in the world of image, health, and fitness, she is frequently featured on *The View*, *Good Morning America*, *Entertainment Tonight*, *Inside Edition*, and *CNN*, and in publications worldwide.